LIVING AN EXCEPTIONAL LIFE

Printed in Canada

ISBN 978-0-9811460-0-3

Library and Archives Canada Cataloguing in Publication

Calvert, C. J., 1975-
Living an exceptional life : powerful strategies to help you take control of your life-- today! / CJ Calvert.

ISBN 978-0-9811460-0-3

1. Self-actualization (Psychology). I. Title.

BF637.S4C344 2008 158.1 C2008-907745-8

LIVING AN EXCEPTIONAL LIFE

POWERFUL STRATEGIES TO HELP YOU TAKE CONTROL OF YOUR LIFE… TODAY!

BY CJ CALVERT

DEDICATION

To **Dr. Steve Stokl**, the greatest mentor I have ever known, the man who taught me to focus my energy, believe in myself, lift up other people and make time for fun: thank you. A person cannot be in your presence without feeling loved, encouraged and sharing in your joy of life. You are an example of who I want to be as a leader, husband and father. To borrow the compliment first offered by your son Zack, if there were a 13th Disciple, you would be it. You are a beloved family man, entrepreneur and community leader, and anyone who is blessed to know you is a better person for it. You are like a second father to me, and I thank you for everything you've done for me.

And to **Scott Cowle**, my Grade 11 English teacher, who challenged me to write a science-fiction short story over one weekend so that I might exempt myself from your exam. You introduced me to a professional writer over dinner because of that story, and birthed in me a dream that one day I could be a published author. Scott, thank you for inspiring that young writer so long ago. You are truly an exceptional teacher, and this book is proof of your positive influence in this student's life.

ACKNOWLEDGEMENTS

"If I have gone farther than other men, it is because I have stood on the shoulders of giants."
- Isaac Newton

I know of no man who is truly *self-made*. We are shaped by our mentors, we are encouraged by our supporters, and we learn from the experiences of those who have gone before us. In the same vein, I know of no author that has crossed the finish line alone. It is almost a cliché within acknowledgments to heap praise upon a mystery team of behind-the-scenes people have banded together to help the author bring the book to life. The reason that it is so popular to praise these wonderful people is that it is *true*. The following remarkable people have all played a pivotal role in bringing this book to life. I wish to thank:

- Jennifer and the team at Volumes publishing for their talent and professionalism;
- My awesome brother Craig Calvert, CG animator for Hollywood blockbusters, for his last-minute work on cover graphics and layout;
- William Meijer for promotional photography;
- My Dad for his proofreading and encouragement;
- My incredible coach and best buddy Tom for keeping me sharp and reminding me to stay on

track with the book; you are a true champion, my friend;

- Steve Stokl for the foreword, and his recommendation to go with Volumes;
- Bill Tibbo for single-handedly opening the door to my entire speaking career; you have changed my life;
- Salim Khoja of The Power Within and David Sersta for offering me the original guidance to get started on this book;
- All my friends and family for their love and support;
- My beautiful son, for being the greatest reason to hold myself accountable to a higher standard of excellence in every area of my life
- And finally my beautiful wife Shannon for proofreading, cheerleading, and being the greatest wife, partner and mom to our beautiful little boy; you are the most incredible human being I know, and my best friend.

TABLE OF CONTENTS

FOREWORD

I'm remembering the joke about the fellow in a bookstore who asks the attendant for assistance with finding the "Self-Help" book section. The attendant, rolling his eyes, says "Well, if I simply told you where it was, that would defeat the purpose, *wouldn't it?!?!"*

The fact is, whether one is motivated by a personal or other person sense of responsibility or simply by a desire to attain strategies to reduce personal suffering of angst, depression, misery, relationship conflict, financial ruin, health compromise, etc., then we do in fact need inspirational, time tested, life-skill guidelines to achieve success. CJ Calvert's book – LIVING AN EXCEPTIONAL LIFE, delivers that prescription. This book is not the medicine for those individuals who want to amble through a life of mediocrity, maintain the status quo, or just cruise with a 'Que Sera, Sera' existence. The words in this read will induce even the most procrastinating temperament given to a 'hardened' state of inertia to take action and improve their overall wellbeing.

When tragedy hits us in our life, as it has (or will) for all of us, often times it is followed by the loss of hope and the unhealthy embracement of despair. Some individuals adopt a lifelong philosophical attitude of, "We are born, we live, we die, and that's it". A ruining acceptance of 'fate' or a destiny to fail starts to grip the mind and prophetically influences their life's outcome.

CJ's own background is one of overcoming, as he perpetually strives to achieve. He has humbled and disciplined himself to seek out mentorship in all areas of his life, to learn from past mistakes, and move on. He has achieved business success, a well-deserved international reputation as a motivational speaker and educator, and has even transformed his physique to hit an award-winning body-building accomplishment along with having challenged his own musical composition and piano skills with a production of two passionate CD's that he has released. As a husband now and father of a one-year-old healthy, handsome boy, he has entered a whole new accountable arena of leading by example. He knows that 'practicing what you preach' is 'walking the talk'. He has also laid out in a very relatable manner, a 'preaching what you practice' method and message which will resonate with any adult reader aspiring for the same perpetual growth and development.

All of us want to go through life with a better attitude, coping and dealing with any sort of stress that comes our way toward a more positive outcome, managing our time and sticking to our priorities, and breathing the benefit of physical health and wellbeing. LIVING AN EXCEPTIONAL LIFE focuses clearly on these issues, underling the balancing of play/work/love and the importance of goal setting and deadlines. After all, none of us are getting out of this life alive in the physical/mental form that we know ourselves. CJ is a great believer that the years represented by the dash between our year of birth and our year of death are more important than the numbers that bookend the inscription on the granite that marks our earthly resting place. It is the quality of how we live our life, our ability to give back and contribute to our loved ones and community, plus the positive difference that we will have made when we make our final exit. This is living an exceptional life and CJ's book captures the key successful principles and how to embrace these habits to reach this mission. I don't know who he was quoting when he stated that he believed the purpose of life was to discover one's talents and then the meaning of life is secured by forever giving those talents away, but CJ's life and his message in this book broadcasts this virtue.

Ansel Adams once said, "There is nothing worse than having a sharp image of a fuzzy picture". So true. None of us want to be a blur. When we have crystallized our belief and lived by golden rule principles, we will deliver a 20-20 view of who we are, what we stand for, and who we have helped along the way. If this is important to you, LIVING AN EXCEPTIONAL LIFE will give you that just reward.

Stephen B. Stokl, M.D., F.R.C.P.(C)
Chief of Psychiatry, Southlake Regional Health Centre
Lecturer, Faculty of Medicine, Department of Psychiatry, University of Toronto
Author of Award Winning book- *Mentally Speaking*

INTRODUCTION

"One man gets nothing but discord out of a piano; another gets harmony. No one claims the piano is at fault. Life is about the same. The discord is there, and the harmony is there. Study to play it correctly, and it will give forth the beauty; play it falsely, and it will give forth the ugliness. Life is not at fault."
-Author Unknown

Every day of our lives, we have a choice to make: whether to pursue excellence in our endeavors, or accept mediocrity as our standard; to embark on the great adventure, or submit to the drudgery of routine; to endure a day that is filled with *excuses*, or celebrate a day that is *extraordinary*.

Our life is the sum of the choices we have made in each moment we face; whether we step up and boldly start that new business, whether we say hello to an attractive stranger in line, whether we get off of the couch and get on the treadmill. The life we are living today is a result of the choices we made yesterday.

If you are in a loveless relationship, you can choose to change it. If you are not satisfied with your career, you can choose to move up or move on. If you look in the mirror and you see a stranger looking back, you can choose to infuse your body with vitality. If you look in you wallet and feel lacking, you can choose to attract prosperity. If you look out the window and feel despair, you can choose to look with different eyes and see hope instead.

Life is rich with choice, and our choices are imbued with a power to alter the entire direction of our life experience. You can decry the hand you're dealt and simply fold, or you can play to win with all you've got. Sticking with the easy path offers immediate comfort and a sense of security; forging a new path invites risk and uncertainty. While most people choose the path of least resistance, I challenge you to choose the path of greatest reward.

I'd like to invite you to join me on a journey, not to find a better place, but to find a better *you*, the best possible version of yourself. We will work together to remove any limiting barriers that are holding you back from enjoying the greatest life experience that you desire and deserve. If you'll allow me, I'd like to share with you some of the things I've learned along my own journey in the hopes that they can open a doorway to new possibilities in your own life.

> ***I'd like to invite you to join me on a journey, not to find a better place, but to find a better you.***
> **-CJ Calvert**

This moment can mark a turning point for you. As you are reading these words, *right now*, you can decide to grab hold of your life with both hands and lift yourself to greater heights. I invite you today to make a bold new choice: to refuse mediocrity and hold yourself to a higher standard of excellence. I invite you to pursue relationships filled with passion, a body filled with strength, and a mind filled with possibility. Don't settle for a life of *ease*; choose instead to create a life that is *exceptional*.

Raise Your Standards

I have enjoyed the pleasure of speaking before literally tens of thousands of audience members over the last decade. It saddens me to meet so many people who want more out of life, but they seem to be caught up in the "rat-race", just trying to make it to Friday and catch their breath. Lots of people are living paycheque-to-paycheque, they aren't physically in the shape they want to be, their relationships are floundering, and they don't know what to do about it.

I'm here to tell you that none of this needs to be your reality. You can make the decision today to step away from the challenges that other people seem to face endlessly. You can choose to take absolute personal responsibility for your life and break out of the limiting habits that have created your reality. You must **raise your standards**: whatever you have accepted before from yourself and the people around you, you can decide to ask more out of life. You know that you are capable of more, and today is the day you can begin to show the world the true talent, energy and genius that has been kept secret within you. You must decide to never again settle for second-best; in order to *get* more out of life, you must *give* more to your life.

As you are reading this, I bet that you desire more for yourself. More passion. More prosperity. More strength. More courage. More peace of mind. You're not looking for someone to just hand you success, because you're willing to do the work... but maybe you're like I was when I hit my brick wall and had no real idea of how to move forward.

I'm going to share with you exactly what happened to me, and exactly what I did to turn my life around. I'm going to walk you through every strategy that I applied to my own life to get the results I enjoy today. Every nugget of wisdom I used to dig myself out of the hole is offered to you here. None of this stuff is theory; this book is like a look inside my daily journal of what I did to turn my life around.

Hitting The Brick Wall

In April of 2002, I was given an incredible gift. It was 4:00 am, on a Saturday, I was at the office, and I was working. All four of these things in combination spelled utter disaster. And the worse part of it was that this behaviour had become the norm for me, rather than the exception. I walked into the office bathroom to splash some cold water on my face, trying anything I could to keep going, and I noticed something disturbing: a huge red mark had appeared across the top left-hand side of my forehead. It was about 3-inches long and an inch thick. It wasn't there yesterday, and now here it was covering half of my face. At first I was shocked, then disgusted… and then I started to get really worried. I didn't know what was happening to me. I felt like I had finally burned out.

You see, at that point, it was pretty standard for me to be working over 100 hours a week. I was waking up at 6:00 am most days, and getting home at midnight every day of the week. Some days I wouldn't even sleep at all, waking up Monday morning and going to bed Tuesday night. I didn't take vacation days; in fact, I had *never* gone on a real vacation as an adult. *Never.* Statutory holidays used to bug me because the only work I could do was paperwork (which I still don't like to this day!). Looking over my bills, I realized that I had spent over $4500 *that year* on Wendy's hamburgers alone. I was living on fast-food and coffee, I wasn't exercising, and to top it off I had eroded many of my most important relationships. Clearly something had to give, and unfortunately what was suffering most obviously was my health. But things hadn't started this way; in fact, what started me on this path was the pursuit of my greatest dreams and goals in life.

You see, when I was 19 years old, my dream career was music performance and composition. I left for university to study orchestral composition so that I could write symphony soundtracks for Hollywood movies. I had put out a pop music tape in record stores through Toronto while I was in high school and enjoyed some modest success with it. My passion truly was music. But I've never been one to conform to someone else's path, and I quickly became disillusioned with my school program; I knew that I needed something more. I figured that if I could just discover a way to make a staggering income, I'd have all the resources I'd need to do anything creative I wanted to do.

I started looking for business opportunities that would help me fulfill my music dreams. I met, befriended and started to work with some very successful people who were driving business to internet websites, a fledgling business at the time which literally exploded in power and scope over the next few years. I immediately saw the potential and partnered with them. Over the next few years, I became a salesman, a sales trainer and eventually a sales motivational speaker, traveling across Ontario and Quebec. By the time I was 24 years old I had led over 300 sales associates, and I was having a great time. But where I was getting lots of accolades for my performance in business, storm clouds were brewing in my personal life.

From 1999-2002, I watched my business go up, and then I watched it start to decline with my declining health, energy and fading humour. I had starved my relationships of time and they simply faded away. I wasn't having fun anymore, which was strange since I absolutely love delivering motivational talks in front of large audiences. The greatest heartbreak of it all was when I realized in the middle of all of this that I had stopped playing the piano, at that point for a couple of *years*. I had no intrinsic interest in internet sales; the only reason I had started on this path was to make money for my music, and I had drifted away from my music completely.

And thus, in April of 2002 I finally hit the brick wall. I had drifted away from my true passion, my health had taken a turn for the worse and I woke up from a daze to realize my life was on the wrong path.

Since I didn't have a family doctor at the time, I grudgingly went to a walk-in clinic to have the doctor on call take a look at me. I had no idea what this big burn mark on my face was: I didn't know if it was cancer, psoriasis, shingles, or hives. The doctor felt that it was probably a "stress rash". I had never heard of this, so he explained that my body wasn't designed to be living in a state of constant stress. The stress response was good for a short burst of energy to get away from a dangerous situation quickly. He used the analogy of needing to pass someone on the highway and dropping the gears on your car from 5th gear to 4th gear in order to accelerate. It's great to do for a few moments of acceleration, but you can't drive on the highway in 4th gear for too long or you'll blow the engine; the engine simply wasn't designed for that amount of stress. Neither was the human body. He said I needed to reduce my stress, get some balance, eat right and exercise, and start having some more fun in my life. If I didn't get some balance immediately, I would be headed for disaster.

A New Beginning

I knew I had to make a change. What I was doing wasn't working. I knew I had to transform my mind, my body, my focus, the way I managed my time, the way I recharged myself. And so, I did what I'm going to encourage you to do: I made a decision to change. We only get one shot at this adventure of life, and I know you're like me: you want to make the most of it.

And so, I've chronicled the strategies that I used to turn myself around in this book. No matter who you are, these principles can be applied to make measurable, lasting change in your life experience.

This book was written for you:

- For every man and woman who has faced the common frustrations of daily living, where every day is filled with irritating lineups, computer malfunctions and traffic jams… instead of seeing what's wrong with your day, you know at some level that having a more **positive attitude** would help you get more juice out of life and enjoy the great moments life has to offer;
- For the busy executive, overwhelmed by **stress,** feeling that the problems you face are so pervasive, so unrelenting, that nothing you do will save you from the pressure cooker that awaits you each day… but you know somehow you've got to find a way to let off some steam;
- For anyone who ever feels like they've spent the whole day putting out fires, only to get home at the end of the day, absolutely exhausted, and yet you feel like you've accomplished NOTHING of importance… but you know if you could simply master your **time** you would get more important things done;
- For everyone who dreamed of doing great things once you graduated, but you woke up 15 years later to realize that things didn't turn out the way you had dreamed they would… you realize that you've got to get clear on what your **goals** are in life: for your health, finances, relationships, career, and every dream still dormant within you;
- For everyone who has faced hardship, setbacks and heartbreak, sometimes situations are so disappointing that we don't even want to try again… but we know that if other people have

overcome obstacles like these, surely we can be inspired by their example;

- For the single mom, struggling to find the time to **exercise**, but exhausted at the end of the day… once the kids are finally in bed, it seems like you don't even have the energy to think, let alone exercise… but you know you need to get in shape;

… to anyone reading these words who yearns for a better quality of life experience: this book was written for you.

I'm writing these words to tell that **it's time**: it's time to take control of your life, to change your attitude, to master you day, to renew your energy, to transform your body, to literally create the life that you've wanted for yourself. It's time to turn this page of your life, and we'll begin this journey together!

CHAPTER 1:

HAVE A POSITIVE ATTITUDE

"The longer I live, the more I realize the impact of attitude on life. Attitude, to me, is more important than facts. It is more important than the past, the education, the money, than circumstances, than failure, than successes, than what other people think or say or do. It is more important than appearance, giftedness or skill. It will make or break a company... a church... a home. The remarkable thing is we have a choice everyday regarding the attitude we will embrace for that day. We cannot change our past... we cannot change the fact that people will act in a certain way. We cannot change the inevitable. The only thing we can do is play on the one string we have, and that is our attitude. I am convinced that life is 10% what happens to me and 90% of how I react to it. And so it is with you... we are in charge of our Attitudes."

- Charles Swindoll

Have you ever wanted to make a positive change in your life, but weren't sure where to start? I'm here to tell you that if you want to make a measurable, powerful improvement in the quality of your daily life experience, there is a simple and immediate step you must take. By taking this one step, you will improve the connection in your relationships, your enjoyment at work, reduce your frustration in times of challenge, boost your immune system, and create a brighter future! This is quite a roster of promises that I offer, with only a single step to take. However, there is a catch: you may have to change the way you view people, the world, and yourself. If you are willing to do so, the quality of your life experience will transcend your wildest expectations.

You have a powerful and secret ability that can allow you, *this moment*, to radically change your life experience for the better! What's amazing about this ability is that you are in complete control. You don't need other people to do nice things for you, or have the sun shine, or see the traffic jam clear up. You don't require your boss giving you a raise, your spouse offering you a compliment, or your kids taking out the garbage.

What is this mysterious ability, this power to transform our life experience? If you want to make an instantaneous change in your life, the one thing that you have complete control over that absolutely affects the quality of your life… is your **attitude**! You can choose to be positive today, right now, and every experience in your life will become more fun, rewarding, and pleasurable. Choose to see the bright side of things, no matter how dire the situation might seem at the time, and the quality of your life instantly improves!

Without question, there are many experiences in life that are out of our control. You might be doing everything right in life, you drive your car through an intersection, and someone else runs the red light and hits your car. Bad things happen to good people all the time. But as German psychiatrist and Holocaust survivor Viktor Frankl said "The last of the human freedoms is to get to choose our attitude under any given set of circumstances." Life is like a roller coaster, going up and coming down, and everyone will continue to experience both good days and bad. But no matter what happens to us, we still have *the choice* to decide how we think and feel about any situation. To quote John Maxwell, **attitude truly is the difference maker!**

> ***"The last of the human freedoms is to get to choose our attitude under any given set of circumstances."***
> **- Viktor Frankl**

Everything Has A Silver Lining... If You Look Hard Enough!

During one of my presentations on managing change, a client approached me to discuss his work situation. He shared with me that his company had just given him the bad news that he, along with thousands of colleagues across the country, were going to be laid off in the next few months. This gentleman, whom we'll refer to as Dan, was understandably distraught. He had felt that his middle-management job was secure, and as the breadwinner of the family he felt that his track to an executive role would pay for his kids' university tuition and secure the family future.

Well, he was so upset that day in late November that he called into work the next morning and told them he needed a mental health day off work; there was no way he could concentrate and get anything accomplished. He felt he needed to clear his head and try to find something to pick up his spirits. He decided to volunteer at his daughter's school that day, thinking that being around the cheerful kids would lift his spirits.

That day, he went to his young daughter's school and helped watch over the kids in the pool. Bob was happy to see his daughter was laughing and splashing in the pool with her friends. But he noticed something unusual: a dark shadow floating at the bottom of the pool. A moment later it registered with him what he was looking at, and he dove fully clothed into the pool to grab a 5-year-old girl that was floating unconscious at the bottom of the pool. He dragged her out of the pool and onto the concrete poolside.

The lifeguard, having seen the splash, had now raced over to help and began CPR and mouth-to-mouth… and was able to save the little girl.

"It's a funny thing, CJ," this man said as he shared the story with me. *"I was so angry and overwhelmed with the loss of my job. It felt so negative to me. But when I think about it, everything has a silver lining if you look hard enough. If I hadn't have been laid off, I wouldn't have gone to my daughters school, I wouldn't have seen the little girl*

drowning, and now there would be a family going into Christmas without their baby with them."

"I'm so glad I got laid off, because I was able to help save that little girl."

I believe that most everyone has experiences that share this lesson, even if they aren't paying attention: that even a very bad situation can sow the seed of a remarkable experience. Think hard about the blessings in your life, and you may find that some of them were born through enduring terrible hardship. And, while the struggle was unpleasant, looking back on things there are many experiences that I would never undue, because they opened the door to the wonderful blessings that I enjoy in my life today.

What Is A Positive Attitude?

A positive attitude is an intellectual decision to look at a situation in the best possible light. In looking to the future, a positive attitude acknowledges the reality of the situation but has an expectancy that the best possible outcome can and will occur. In looking at the past, a positive attitude only reviews setbacks and failures as "learning and growth opportunities" and does not needlessly review them masochistically. Some people just like to review bad experiences over and over again in their mind. What's the point of that, aside from learning and improving? Reviewing the video in your mind of a horrible day just makes you feel horrible over and over again!

A positive attitude does NOT deny the reality of the situation. If you are driving through an intersection and someone runs the red light and hits you, you have had an accident. A positive attitude doesn't whistle cheerfully and say *"Nothing happened!"* That isn't being *positive*; that's being *delusional*. What a positive attitude does is it takes the situation and imagines that things will work out alright in the end. A negative attitude, however, will say "Our car is destroyed! The insurance company probably won't pay! I'll have to walk to work! I'll get home at 9pm and won't ever see my kids before they go to sleep!" This is using your imagination to project the worst possible outcome. A positive attitude says "Wow. Will you look at that? My car has had been hit. Well, at least my family and I are safe and healthy, the insurance will certainly cover this… everything is fine.

My wife and I went through a situation last year buying a house. We literally looked at over 800 houses on the internet and we estimate we physically walked through over 3 dozen. Our real estate agent was very friendly, but we imagined that we must be pushing her to her limits when after a year of looking we still hadn't purchased a house. We actually asked her once what the typical experience was and what was considered an average number for the number of houses you walk through. She smiled and said "The average couple walks through between three to five houses." We had gone through dozens of houses at that point!

After a year of this, we find a place that we think might meet our needs. I can only imagine how excited our agent was! We put an offer on the house, but five minutes later we got the phone call… the house had been bought. Now, a negative attitude would say "Oh, that's just great! We'll NEVER find the house we're looking for! This will go on for YEARS!" But my wife and I looked at each other and immediately said "Well, the next house we see will probably be even better than this one!" And it was, and we bought it... and it is a gold-plated palace compared to the first house on which we put an offer! That's what a positive attitude does. You imagine things will turn out alright. A negative view will say "Great, it's probably going to rain today... the day is ruined!" But a positive view would say "It might rain today, but I'll be prepared with an umbrella just in case. Either way, I've decided to have a great day!"

What Is The Value In Having A Positive Attitude?

"A great attitude does much more than turn on the lights in our worlds; it seems to magically connect us to all sorts of serendipitous opportunities that were somehow absent before the change."
- Earl Nightingale

Since many people struggle with having a positive attitude, you must wonder why it isn't a greater priority. I'm definitely not perfect, and I'll admit that I certainly have days where my attitude needs to be adjusted; but I assure you that there is rarely any value in having a negative attitude. You make more money when you have a positive attitude. You have a better marriage with a positive attitude. You strengthen your immune system, fend off illness, attract quality people and relationships and navigate through challenging life situations with grace, ease and power when you have a positive attitude.

If you were a manager and you had two employees, both of whom had the same level of experience, the same work ethic, and even produced the same volume and quality of work… but one of them was a joy to work with and the other one was a suffering, torturous pessimist… with whom would you prefer to work? If one of them was appreciative, kind, respectful, pleasant, agreeable, had a great team spirit, and thought well of you and the company, why wouldn't you want that one around more? If you're anything like me, I find negative people draining. Frankly, I am very successful at keeping negative people far away from me. It's exhausting to be in their presence and listen to them complain all the time! So, a positive attitude is a major key in keeping you marketable and promotable in your career.

In fact, there aren't many situations where you would not benefit immeasurably from having a positive attitude. You can apply this to your health, your finances, your career, your marriage… everything will benefit from a positive attitude. A colleague of mine shared this story with me about a conversation on the value of having a positive attitude:

A motivational speaker was sitting on an airplane next to a grumpy man. They exchanged cursory greetings, and while waiting for the plane to taxi out onto the runway, a conversation started over what each man did for a living. When he shared that he was a positive-thinking motivational speaker, the other man snorted in retort.

"Motivational stuff is for the birds", the grumpy man said. "It doesn't work anyway".

The motivational speaker was curious about this statement and asked the grumpy man to explain what he meant. "Why don't you think positive thinking works?" asked the speaker. The grumpy man thought about his words before answering.

"Because it doesn't last," he finally said. "I've been to lots of those 'positive attitude' meetings, and sure! They get you all fired up that evening. But the next day you wake up, and all that positive attitude and excitement has worn off. It DOESN'T LAST, so it's just a big waste of time." The speaker nodded in understanding before answering.

"You know, I appreciate how you feel," the speaker began. "However, I've discovered something in life. Most of the important things in life don't last; they need to be worked on everyday in order to renew them. For example, this morning I took a shower. Now, I think by tonight I will have discovered that the shower DIDN'T LAST. Despite that I've learned in life that it's still probably a good idea to have a shower, every day!"

HOW ARE EMOTIONS CREATED?

"In between stimulus and response, there is a gap. The key to both our growth and happiness is how we use that gap."
- Stephen Covey

I have exciting news for you! You have complete control over your emotional experience. However, I have potentially bad news: You have complete control over your emotional experience. This can be either a liberating thought (if you have a sense of responsibility and a proactive nature) or this can be a debilitating thought (if you like to blame others for your misfortune and lack the maturity to be personally responsible.)

I run into a number of people who have struggled with 'anger management' and feel very uplifted that they have attended classes to give them tools to control their emotions more effectively. But it is disappointing to see that managing their anger means *not acting in an angry way*: not yelling or swearing, not waving their fists in the air, not hitting things or people. While this is a commendable improvement over their past behavior, unfortunately while they no longer *act* angry, they certainly still *feel* angry. They've forced a smile on their face and swallowed their tongue, but inside they are still steaming, filled with venomous rage and plotting revenge against their oppressors.

Wouldn't it be a remarkable trick if you could flip a switch in your brain and not even feel angry? To literally cancel the emotion on the outset and simply feel calm, relaxed and cheerful? No need to put on an appearance of civility and strain to keep your tongue in check; you just don't feel upset anymore. I'm convinced that if people would just get serious about taking responsibility for managing their emotions, the hatred and violence in this world could be brought to a halt.

This sounds like a neat trick, doesn't it? Here's how it works. With practice, you can train your brain to do exactly what I'm describing:

STIMULOUS: In any situation, first there is a trigger or event that may set you off: you pour hot coffee on your lap; you are leaving your home later than you had planned; you are caught in a traffic jam; the lineup at the grocery store is longer than you would prefer; someone interrupts your presentation to the sales team, etc.

RESPONSE: A moment after the stimulus, you have a response: How do you feel? What do you say/do? What is your reaction?

But in between the stimulus and the response, there is a moment where you have total control. You see, our brain soaks in all of the data (visual, auditory, kinesthetic, etc.) and has to interpret the data to make sense of what it is experiencing. A split second after you experience the stimulus, your brain asks a very powerful question: WHAT DOES THIS MEAN? So, our thought process looks like this:

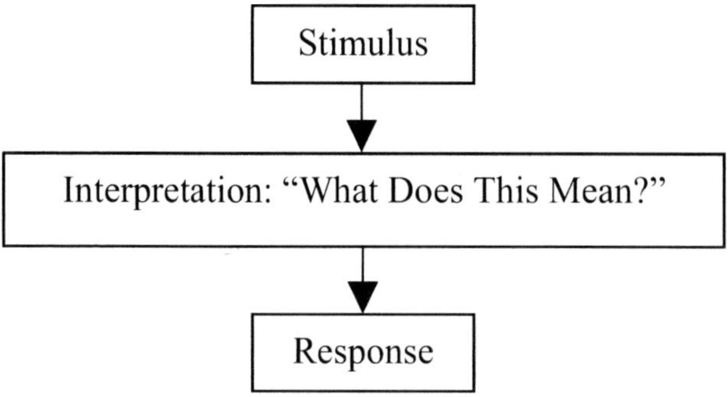

Allow me to share one of my own examples. I have a major pet peeve with people who speed and change lanes aggressively. I think it's dangerous and it puts other motorists at risk. Well, one day years ago I was driving on the highway and little blue 2-door hatchback raced past me, weaved in and around traffic at high speeds, and I said to myself: *"That thoughtless teenage punk; he doesn't care if he hurts other people. He just likes to speed recklessly."* I could feel myself getting angry. A moment later the little blue hatchback was followed at high speeds by a gold-colored 4-door sedan. I *thought "There goes another punk, chasing his little friend around, having a street race on the highway."* I don't know who I was angrier with at the time. I certainly felt that the gold sedan should slow down and back off; I thought maybe they could be rival gang members.

Now, consider the stages of what was going on in my mind. At the first stage, STIMULUS, I watched the cars drive by very quickly and weave through traffic. A few moments later, I felt the emotion called 'anger'. But in between the stimulus and the response, there was a moment where my brain had to interpret the data that I was collecting, and arrive at a conclusion. My brain asked "What does this mean?" The answer I came with was *"The driver of the car is a thoughtless punk who doesn't care if he puts innocent people in danger; he is so selfish."*

The power in understanding this process is that you come to realize that **your INTERPRETATION of the situation is what creates your emotional response, NOT the situation itself**.

Is it possible that I don't have all of the data? Absolutely. Is it possible that if I had all of the information, I might think and feel differently about the situation? Absolutely. Is it possible that my mind is filling in the blank and just GUESSING what is going on, and that I am treating my guess as if were and actual FACT? Absolutely. People forget that their interpretations and guesses are only that: just guesses. In this example, I did not know the intentions of the driver or who they were. I was making a huge mental leap and assuming that it was, in my words, a thoughtless teenage punk. But is that a fact that I was certain of? No, I was making an assumption. Did I know the drivers intentions? Again, no.

> ***Your INTERPRETATION of the situation is what creates your emotional response, NOT the situation itself.***

Consider this same scenario: what if I drove up beside the little blue car and saw that it was a pregnant mother racing to the hospital to give birth. What if it was a volunteer firefighter trying to get to the station, or a surgeon racing to save someone's life? Would this change the reason for why they were speeding, and therefore change my interpretation of the facts? Yes, absolutely. If it were pregnant women, I wouldn't feel angry; I would feel concern, because in my mind I would be saying "Oh, I hope she gets to the hospital in time, safely."

By the way, in the story of the two cars on the highway, the gold 4-door sedan was an unmarked police car, chasing down the speeding Honda Civic driver!

Choose a Better Interpretation of Events

"Between the optimist and the pessimist, the difference is droll. The optimist sees the doughnut; the pessimist the hole!"
-Mclandburgh Wilson

"... unless you are Tim Horton's donuts, and you make a ton of profit on Timbit donut-holes!"
- (my wife, Shannon Jackson, in response to the above quote!)

Another example of this occurred during a training seminar I had conducted with a major power company. I was training a group of middle-managers, and one participant put up her hand. We'll call her Barb.

Barb explains *"CJ, I've got a colleague named Sandy who drives me crazy." I asked "What does Sandy do?" Barb took a deep breath and explained. She said "For example, last week Sandy calls me at 9am and says 'Hey Barb, is the XYZ report finished yet?' To which I reply, 'No Sandy, it will be done by 5pm as we agreed.' Sandy says 'Hey no problem, Barb,' and she hangs up the phone."*

"Well, wouldn't you know it but 30 minutes later she calls back and asks again 'Hey Barb, is the report done?' I

say 'No Sandy, it'll be done by 5pm like I said before' and she says 'No problem' and hangs up."

"10 o'clock she phones and asks 'Is the report done?' 10:30 she phones; 'Is the report done?' 11am, 'Are you finished?' 11:30 'Is it ready', etc etc ALL DAY LONG."

I ask the middle manager why she thinks Sandy is doing this. Barb answers: *"It's obvious: SHE'S AN IDIOT! And, she's trying to drive me insane."* I ask if there is any other possible reason that she might be doing this, and Barb can't think of one example. This is a perfect illustration of how Stimulus - Interpretation - Response works. Barb had locked onto one possible interpretation - that Sandy is calling to deliberately bother her - and Barb is blind to the possibility that there might be another explanation.

So, is there a possibility that there might be another explanation for Sandy's behavior, one that would make it understandable, tolerable and non-frustrating to us? Yes, but it is up to us to do the mental work to conceive of the alternative. We get the mental ball rolling by asking our brain the question: What ELSE could this mean? Another way to ask this question might be: Under what circumstances would this behavior be acceptable to me? I ask the group to brainstorm some alternative explanations as to why Sandy might be calling back every 30 minutes. Here are some examples:

- Sandy does not realize she is being a pest; she is simply curious about the progress of the work
- Sandy has been told by her own manager to phone Barb over and over until the report is

handed in. Sandy is very embarrassed to phone but she is under orders.

- Sandy has learned the hard way that Barb is absolutely disorganized and that they ONLY WAY to get Barb to do things on time is to phone her, over and over. Barb is blind to her own inadequacies and blames the people around her for their behavior
- Sandy needs the report before 5pm, but is embarrassed to say this directly to Barb. Perhaps because Sandy has made a mistake and told Barb the wrong deadline, or made some other similar error. However, instead of owning up to her mistake, Sandy choosing instead to bother and cajole Barb into action by phoning over and over.
- Maybe Sandy has short term memory loss; she literally forgets that she had the conversation 30 minutes ago! Unlikely, but it has happened.

The opportunity for Barb in this situation is to manage her own perception. Instead of simply getting angry, she can choose to perceive the intentions behind Sandy's actions differently, and Barb can immediately let off some stress and be more effective in her day.

Personally, if I can't think of a positive perception, I will choose to use a generic thought such as "Maybe I don't have all of the information." At least I'm not jumping to conclusions!

Sometimes participants ask me *"CJ, why not just simply ASK Sandy why she is doing this?"* This is a very good question. It would seem that, at first glance, the easiest thing to do would be to ask. However, if you've already jumped to conclusions and assumed that Sandy is behaving badly for negative reasons, you could still ask Sandy WHY she behaves as she does, but your tone of voice and body language will betray your actual thoughts. Even if you use nice words, you will still sound irritated with Sandy. Thus, you need to calm yourself down FIRST, before you approach someone with questions. You need to have a calm, open-minded spirit, and the person will be able to converse with you much more effectively. Asking these positive questions allows you to calm down so that you can talk to one another.

Perception is Reality

"When you look at the world in a narrow way, how narrow it seems! When you look at it in a mean way, how mean it is! When you look at it selfishly, how selfish it is! But when you look at it in a broad, generous, friendly spirit, what wonderful people you find in it."
- Horace Rutledge

How does perception work? All of your experience of reality is filtered through your perception. Think of perception as the view of the world that you might see through the lens of a camera. It is up to you to point the camera where you see fit. The camera will delete all else from view, focusing only on what you choose. If you choose to point your camera at a sunset, you see beauty. If you choose to point your camera at a car wreck, you see tragedy. The power in perception is that it is completely under your control as to which direction you point the camera.

However, another variable comes into play. Two people can be pointing their camera at the same exact image and have a different experience looking at it. The classic positive attitude question remains "Do you see the glass as half empty or half full?" Both subjects are looking at the exact same situation, yet their perception will twist reality to suit their attitude. The pessimist sees the glass as half-empty. The optimist sees the glass as half-full. The eternal optimist sees the glass as completely full: Half water and half air!

How is this possible? Because you must view reality through the lens of the camera, and *we* are the lens. *Anais Nin says "We don't see things as* they *are, we see things as* we *are."* The lens on your camera is made up of your beliefs, your personality, your experiences, and your emotional state at the moment. One person may have a wide-angle lens that distorts reality and stretches the truth. One person may have a telephoto lens that zooms in on the smallest possible detail, making things seem bigger than they really are, thereby creating a "mountain out of a molehill". The lens may be "rose-tinted" and exaggerate the benefits of a situation.

What if the lens has a scratch in it? More importantly, what if you don't realize that the scratch exists? Consider what would happen. Every picture you took would have a scratch on it. Every person you meet, every situation you see, would harbor the same negative scratch. And, if you were not aware that the lens even exists, you would believe that

> *"We don't see things as* **they** *are, we see things as* **we** *are."*
> **- Anais Nin**

the people whom you meet have a scratch on them. If your lens has a scratch of hatred, you will see every action a person takes as an attack on you and you will desire retaliation. If your lens has been polished to perceive fairness, you will see honesty and integrity in your dealings with people.

TOOLS FOR MANAGING YOUR ATTITUDE

Ask Positive Questions

The challenge for most people is that they focus their camera on the 1% of the situation that is negative, instead of the 99% of the situation that is wonderful. They see only the difficulties and not the reward.

You must focus your lens on the best possible angle of any situation. To do this, must utilize the power of your Reticular Activating System. Your RAS is the part of your brain that tells you what is important to notice, and what is irrelevant and should be ignored. Since we are inundated with billions of bits of sensory information all through the day, it would be impossible to direct any meaningful level of attention on everything. To manage this onslaught of information, your brain systematically deletes most of the sensory data from conscious perception. You simply ignore most of what is going on around you, and pay attention only to the things you deem worthwhile.

A common example of this is when you purchase a new car. As soon as you are on the road, you begin to notice multiple copies of your car model driving on the road that did not appear before today! Did everyone go out the same day and buy the same car? No; the cars were always there. It's just that your brain hadn't told you that the car was significant enough to notice, so you deleted the information from conscious perception. Since the car is now significant to you, your brain sends a wake-up call to your RAS and you now see the car that was in front of you the entire time.

Another example would be when you walk into a room. Depending upon your profession, you will see different things in the identical setting. If you are a fire fighter, you will immediately notice whether or not there is a sprinkler system, fire extinguisher, a clear escape route, if the door is blocked, if the room is dangerously overcrowded, etc. If you are an interior designer, your focus will look to the colour scheme, the layout of furniture, the choice of fabrics and textures, the lighting, and the overall "statement" that the room makes. The exact same room will offer a different experience from one person to the next.

It is important to note at this point that your RAS is a critical tool in shaping success, because it awakens you to opportunities that you may not have noticed before. If your mind is focused on real estate, you will see "For Sale" signs, real estate literature and listings that other people simply don't bother to notice. Your ears will lock onto any mention of a foreclosure or "power of sale" that is mentioned casually in conversation. If you are in sales, you will take note of the business and professions of the people you meet and be aware of new opportunities to market your product. You will have your antennae up and notice new relationships that could be formed. Your RAS will highlight opportunities that go unnoticed by others, even if those opportunities are right in front of their nose. Because your brain has told your RAS that these opportunities are significant, you can move quickly and take action.

EXAMPLES OF POSITIVE QUESTIONS:

- **What is GREAT about this situation?**
- **What is FUNNY about this situation?**
- **What am I GRATEFUL for in this situation?**
- **What can I learn from this?**
- **How will this make me stronger?**
- **What opportunities will come from this?**
- **How is this making things harder for my competition?**
- **What strengths do I have that give me an advantage in this situation?**
- **Will this make a great story in years to come?**
- **Why is it better that this is happening to ME than to other people?**
- **Why is it better that this is happening HERE vs. somewhere else?**
- **Why is it better that this is happening NOW rather than later?**

Positive Reframing: "What Is GREAT About This Situation?"

"They've got us surrounded again, the poor bastards."
- *Creighton Abrams,* United States Army General

No matter what the situation is, there is always an opportunity to find a silver lining. Sometimes, the positive aspect of the situation may be very difficult to see right away. In fact, it is extremely useful to ask the question 'What's GREAT about this situation?' Here are some examples:

Situation:	"My 7-year-old car just broke down… that's terrible!!!"
What's Great:	"Now, I can get a new car!"
Situation:	"This lineup in the grocery store is so long… I can't stand it!
What's Great:	"Thank goodness there IS a grocery store, and that I didn't have to *grow* the food!"
Situation:	"My job has me work all of the major holidays!"
What's Great:	"If I don't like my in-laws, now I don't have to see them!"
Situation:	"My auto insurance went up to $8000 a year!"
What's Great:	"At least I still get to DRIVE!"

Consider the following statements and the examples provided, and create your own responses!

Situation:	"My phone at work rings off the hook… I never have break!"
What's Great:	________________________________
Situation:	"The power at our home went out over the weekend!"
What's Great:	________________________________
Situation:	"I'm stuck in a huge traffic jam on the highway!"
What's Great:	________________________________

Now, consider the negative thought about some situations that you've been facing. Take a moment and try to re-write them into a highly positive outlook.

Situation:

____

What's Great:

____

Situation:

____

What's Great:

____

Situation:

____

What's Great:

____

One day while delivering training on positive attitude to a manufacturing firm, I had a very negative audience member sitting in on my session. No matter what advice I tried to share, he discounted all of it. We were talking about having a positive attitude on the job when he put up his had to complain again.

He said *"CJ, I've got something here at work that really bothers me."* *I forced myself to keep a smile on my face and said, "Go ahead, Bob. Please share."*

He goes on to describe his situation. He says *"Well, I sit at my desk and the phone rings. No problem, right? Well I pick up the phone and say hello, I talk with the person and take some notes, then I hang up the phone."* He stopped talking, and I asked him where he was going with this. His face got a look of exasperation.

"The problem is, the minute I hang up the phone, it rings again! Immediately, with no break. So I pick it up again," he says, sounding irritated just describing the situation, "And I answer it and take notes and hang up… and it rings again! Right away, with no break! It's just a ceaseless barrage of ringing! My phone just rings and rings off the hook all day long! I don't have time for a drink of

water or food or a cigarette or even to catch my breath! So, CJ, what's so 'positive' about that, huh?"

I considered what he had said and after a moment I said *"Wow, I can really hear the frustration in your voice as you describe this; this must feel very unfair and overwhelming for you. Tell me,"* I asked, *"why are they people calling you over and over?"*

He looks me straight in the eye and says, deadpan, *"The reason my phone is ringing off the hook all day? The reason they won't leave me alone? Oh… the reason they keep calling me… is to* place orders!"

There is a LOT of irony in a salesperson's complaint that the phone is ringing off the hook with people wanting to buy your product! Instead of complaining about being so busy, this man should be thankful that he has such incredible job security!

HUMOR: "What Is FUNNY About This Situation?"

"A person without a sense of humour is like a wagon without springs -- jolted by every pebble in the road."
- Henry Ward Beecher

Humour is a tremendously powerful tool, rendering embarrassing situations tolerable and stressful situations less dramatic. It has the effect of reducing our imaginary mountains into their rightful molehills. I've found in life that the people with the ability to laugh at themselves and the situations they face are able to meet life with a joyous sense of discovery, fun and adventure, rather than facing life with apprehension and fear. When we ask the question "What's funny about this situation", our mind searches for the humour in our experience and will more likely to find an answer.

Laughter is a powerful stress-relieving tool. When we laugh, our body produces a neuro-transmitter called 'endorphins'. Endorphins are released by behaviour such as laughter, are 100 times more powerful than morphine and have the same chemical structure as morphine. During times of physical discomfort, they block the pain signal from reaching the brain. As well, they make you feel happy! Stress and anxiety are reduced or eliminated. If we are able to find a way to laugh at the situations we are in, they are much easier to endure.

> ***Endorphins are 100 times more powerful than morphine and have the same chemical structure as morphine.***

Laughter also helps combat disease. Dr Norman Cousins was afflicted with a deadly form of arthritis. His family doctor told him that his days were numbered. Dr Cousins decided to test a hypothesis that he had been contemplating: that massive doses of laughter would have a powerful and positive impact on your immune system, and aid in the prevention and treatment of disease. Dr Cousins locked himself in a hotel room, took massive doses of Vitamin C, and focused on love, happiness, gratitude and laughter. He watched Marx Brothers comedy movies all day long for weeks on end. He found that even 10 minutes of laughter would give him up to two-hours of pain-free sleep. As well, the motion of belly laughing seemed to loosen up the tension and discomfort in his spine and work to counteract the arthritis. When he returned for a check up, his family doctor was stunned to discover that the disease was in remission. Dr Norman Cousins went on to share his pioneering discovery about the healing power of laughter in his landmark book, "Anatomy of an Illness".

The next time you are in a tense situation, try to poke light fun at the situation... you might find that it relieves some of your tension and puts a positive spin on your predicament! I remember years ago when I was just getting started as a professional speaker that I was running late for a presentation. You must appreciate that the cardinal sin of speaking is canceling a presentation at the last moment for any reason, and the second-greatest sin is being late. Your audience is sitting there, waiting for the show to begin! Well, I was running late, and I must confess that I was driving somewhat aggressively to reach my goal. Wouldn't you know it, but I looked up into my rear-view mirror to see the flashing lights of a police car, pulling me over for speeding!

The timing couldn't be worse. I was already so tense and worried about being late, and getting a ticket was going to put me behind schedule even more. It seemed like the officer couldn't have moved more slowly! I almost wanted to give him my wallet and ask to pay by the roadside, just so that I could leave. Exasperated, I politely asked him to please hurry, and that I was really running late.

He smiled and said "I thought you were in a rush. What's so important that you're running late for?"

"I've got to do a presentation and the audience is waiting for me!", I replied tensely.

"Wow! What do you do professionally?" He asked.

"I'm a professional speaker, and I'm really late now!"

"That's really interesting!" he commented. *"What are you speaking on?"* I paused, and finally answered:

"I'm giving a presentation… on being better at TIME MANAGEMENT!"

GRATITUDE: "Why am I so LUCKY that this is happening?"

"Both abundance and lack exist simultaneously in our lives, as parallel realities. It is always our conscious choice which secret garden we will tend ... when we choose not to focus on what is missing from our lives but are grateful for the abundance that's present-love, health, family, friends, work, the joys of nature, and personal pursuits that bring us pleasure -- the wasteland of illusion falls away and we experience heaven on earth."
- Sarah Ban Breathnach

For some reasons, it seems easier for most people to focus on what isn't working well in their lives. We are so focused on what we don't have, compared to the next guy, but as soon as we get what we want, we complain about why it isn't perfect! If you are taking the bus, all you complain about is that you don't have a car. As soon as you have a car, you notice it doesn't have power windows. When you've got power windows, you notice that you don't have a DVD player for the kids. When you get that, you notice that you don't have voice-activated GPS and Bluetooth for your cellphone! It's absolutely amazing how we complain about what we don't have!

I love standing in the "8-item or less" express line at a grocery store. You really get to watch human nature in action. Someone in front of you puts down 9 items, and you only have to count the seconds before another person in line gets bent out of shape over it. In fact, I was standing in line one time where an irritated patron, with steam literally rising off her scalp, said to the offender: "Did you miss the day in Grade 1 where they covered the difference between the number 8 and the number 9?" Or if someone is in line at McDonald's, and it is 10:31 am, and McDonald's has STOPPED making breakfast Egg McMuffins. This seems to be a cataclysmic catastrophe for the poor soul who has the happiness of their entire morning hanging on whether or not they consume an Egg McMuffin. Surely, we can aspire to higher standards of excellence in life that getting frustrated over not getting our morning McMuffin!

One of the greatest gifts you can give yourself is the quiet pause of reflection; simply stopping to consider every blessing that you enjoy in your life. When times seem troubling, it helps to consider everything good for which we have to be thankful. We are never more aware of how lucky we are to be able to walk, than when we see another unfortunate soul in a wheelchair beside us. And yet, the person in the wheelchair, with the proper mental attitude, may have a more rewarding life than ours simply because they choose to focus on the fact that they can still see the sunset, hear a symphony or the words "I love you", taste chocolate, hold the hand of their loved ones and smell the roses along life's journey.

Using gratitude as a tool for managing our emotions is a very popular coping mechanism in a hospital when someone faces a serious injury. Rather than focus on the injury, the person can look to the bed beside them and say "Wow, I lost my hand in the car accident, but the guy beside me has become paralyzed. I'm so lucky to be alive!"

I keep a newspaper article in my office, scotch-taped to the wall. It's a story of a farmer from Ontario, who several years ago lost his 7 children, and his wife who was pregnant with their eighth child, in a fire that eradicated his home and his family in one night. The photo is of the farmer holding the white casket of his little 18-month old baby in his arms and placing her in the ground. This isn't a happy picture, and it doesn't lift me up; rather, it offers perspective. You see, any day I come home and I feel like I've had a "tough day" and I feel a little down, I need only look at that photograph and the tragedy that this poor man faced and realize how incredibly blessed that I am. I have absolutely ZERO real problems in my life.

I try as often as possible to shift my focus towards what I am grateful for in my life, as opposed to what isn't yet in my life. Here are some of my thoughts of what I'm grateful for.

Things I'm grateful for:

- Being alive
- Being healthy and free of disease; able to walk, talk, hear music, taste chocolate, hold my baby boy in my arms and kiss my wife. Able to think and contemplate ideas, to learn new skills
- I am grateful for my wife, who is the most courageous human being I know, who is so brilliant and knowing exactly the right words to

say in any situation, and constantly encourages me to pursue my dreams. She was born to be a mom to our beautiful boy. She was destined for this new career, despite being adored by every employee she leads and client she brilliantly serves in her work

- I am grateful for my son who is the greatest source of joy in my life, for whom I have discovered unconditional love, whom I would lay my life down for; I would trade anything in my life to keep him safe and healthy
- I am grateful for my incredibly family and friends who are a constant blessing and source of fun and support in my life
- I am grateful to live in Canada, this amazing free nation; I can vote for who I want, I am free to go where I want, to practice whatever religion, marry who I want, work at what I want, and despite paying a lot of tax I can earn whatever I want
- I am grateful to my great friend Bill Tibbo who opened the door to my professional speaking career years ago. He has changed my life forever. I love my career, the opportunities given to me with what I do. I feel more alive on stage than anywhere else!
- I am grateful to my parents who helped shape me into the person I am today
- I am grateful to my dear mentor for many years, Dr Steve Stokl, who guided me in learning everything I know today about success thinking, leading people and building business teams

- I am grateful to my high-school teachers Ian Hoare, Tom Gough, Scott Cowle and Richard Bramwell who each left an indelible mark for good in my life
- I love technology and how it allows me to enjoy my music, and create movies of my baby boy and share them with friends and family; I love that I can stay connected with my awesome brother Craig, Emma and baby nephew Kaden

Now that I've shared some of the things I'm grateful for, take a moment and consider how this same question applies to you: what are all the things in your life that you are grateful for, or could be? Take a few moments and write them down.

WHAT ARE YOU GRATEFUL FOR?

1. ____________________________________
2. ____________________________________
3. ____________________________________
4. ____________________________________
5. ____________________________________

If you want to transform your life, start every day and say, out loud, everything that you are grateful for. It immediately changes your perspective, puts you in a great mood, and arms you for any challenge the day might offer!

Change your Vocabulary!

"Please God, make my words today sweet and tender, for tomorrow I may have to eat them."
- Author Unknown

Men have shaped history with the power of their words. Words have the ability to inspire action or deflate enthusiasm. We have total control over how we describe the world and our experiences to ourselves. The words that we choose to represent our experience can actually affect how we perceive reality.

You can recognize an individual with a negative, defeatist attitude simply by listening to the words they choose. A Chinese Proverb says ***"If you wish to know the mind of a man, listen to his words."*** Powerful, success-minded individuals have infused their vocabulary with words that inspire confidence and action. In his inaugural speech, President John F Kennedy says "Ask not what your country can do for you; ask what you can do for your country!", and a nation is inspired.

> ***"If you wish to know the mind of a man, listen to his words."***
> **- Chinese Proverb**

Years ago, I learned this lesson and began doing some housecleaning on my personal vocabulary. One of the words that I have successfully stifled in my own speech is the word "problem". Very consistently, when faced with what others would describe as a 'problem' I choose to use the word "challenge".

Whenever something doesn't go my way, it's a "learning opportunity". And when things get really exciting, I quote motivational speaker Les Brown and **say "I didn't have a bad day today, I had a CHARACTER-BUILDING day!"**

What I've discovered is that using a positive word can instantly change how I feel about the situation. Instead of feeling discouraged I feel energized and hopeful. I keep my good humour and sense of expectancy. But most people use the power of words to magnify their negative emotions. For example, when people drive aggressively or in a state of anger, we refer to the cause of their behavior as "Road Rage". I'm sure you've heard this term before. Imagine what it does to the driver when they are locked in the grip of their negative emotions behind the wheel. First of all, it gives them psychological permission to behave badly, since they don't feel that they have ownership in their behavior; after all, they are in the grip of "Road Rage" and their reactions are understandable and excusable.

> ***"I didn't have a bad day today, I had a CHARACTER-BUILDING day!"***
> **- Les Brown**

But secondly, the word "Rage" is such an intense word. I think it gives them permission to react even more angrily than before the term was invented. Imagine if instead of the term "Road Rage", we used a term that made the driver feel foolish about themselves, like "Road *Ridiculousness*". How about "Road *Goofiness*" or "Road *Silliness*"? Some people might think twice before driving so poorly again!

Just by changing the words, we can diminish or heighten our emotion about the event. So many people are blasé in their morning introductions. When asked

"How are you?" many people will simply respond by saying "Fine". If you want to magnify your energy level and your representation of the world to yourself, why not answer "I'm fantastic!" or "I'm an unstoppable tidal wave of success!" When someone makes a request of you, instead of saying "Sure" in a dull monotone, why not say *"Absolutely! That would be amazing! I'd be thrilled to do that! What an exciting opportunity!"* You might find that by replacing your old words with some new positive energized words, it feels a little silly and over the top at first. Great! You've succeeded in putting a bit of a smile on your face. The other thing that happens is that you will stand out in a crowd. It's hard not to take notice of someone with such an indomitable spirit.

The opposite is also true. Just as magnifying your positive words will increase your positive emotions, softening the intensity of your negative words will soften the intensity of your negative emotions. If you receive news that is not encouraging, instead of saying "this is AWFUL", say *"this is interesting. This is a fascinating plot twist. My, how the universe keeps me on my toes! I can't wait to find out what's going to happen next!"* Instead of saying "I'm so FURIOUS; I'm going to KILL him!" Say, "my feathers have been ruffled, and I'm going to send a strongly worded memo!" If someone had done something negative, instead of saying "I feel BETRAYED!" say "I'm feeling a bit let down. That's not the way I had hoped things would turn out. Well, things could be a lot worse than they are."

Pay attention to the words you use on a regular basis. Are they too intensely negative? If so, do some mental housecleaning and make a concerted effort to change your behavior. In the beginning, select a positive phrase that can stand in as an alternative to the negative words you may have used before. If you catch yourself slipping back into the old pattern of negative language, just stop yourself and say "Oh, what I meant to say was…" and use the new affirming words you've selected. You'll find in no time at all with some work and creativity on your part that a lot of the negative language driving your representation of reality gets updated for the better!

Change the Channel

The human mind functions much like any machine: as a piece of technology, it will follow the instructions you give it. Most men and women, unaware of the power of suggestion upon their own mind, unfortunately allow a lifetime of contradictions and crippling philosophies to run wild, wrecking havoc on their subconscious and ultimately on the achievements they hope to produce.

One young man dreams of opening his own bakery, yet remembers how his father told him "Don't rise above your raisings". Since the father has struggled all of his life to make ends meet for the family, the man believes at some level that to have a successful business would be a direct insult to his father. Because of this, he holds himself back from taking the fateful plunge into entrepreneurship.

Another young man dreams of being married. He has enjoyed a wonderful relationship with his girlfriend over the past few years. When asked, he would tell you that he believes that he has a tremendous amount to offer his potential bride, he believes in family as the greatest social institution, and wants the emotional stability that companionship could bring. However, this young man watched his parents suffer a bitter divorce and faced great sadness through his childhood. When several of his colleagues at work file for divorce from their wives, the young man breaks up with his girlfriend. Despite the fact that they were happy, he shrugs and says "Well, everyone gets divorced. It's just a matter of time before we do to." His belief system has been marred, and his behavior reflects it.

Our mind is capable of creating whatever image we choose, but most people are not aware that they can choose what their mind focuses on and manifests.

Think of your mind like a television set. When you turn it on to one channel, all you see are re-runs of all of your failures, all of your embarrassing moments, every injustice that has been leveled against you, every moment of sadness and pain that you've endured. Watching all of this would be overwhelmingly negative, and I would ask you: "What would you do?"

Well, most people would turn off the television. Since it's the source of your pain, just shut it down. But the problem is that it is very nearly impossible to think of NOTHING. To blank out your mind is incredibly difficult; if I say to you "Don't think of a stuffed pink fuzzy bunny", your mind ignores the word "Don't" and simply imagines the pink fuzzy bunny.

The very best solution when your mind is churning out a stream of negativity and filth is to simply CHANGE THE CHANNEL. Put something positive and uplifting on the television! Something humorous, fun, energizing or inspiring. Now your subconscious has something tangible to chew on, and it will retain the positive images and replace the negative images.

What 'Channel' are YOU Watching?

1. **Negative PAST Focus**. Saying things like "I've never been good at that, I always been a loser." You review the movies of all of your disasters, making them bigger and louder than life, focusing on the most hurtful elements. By reviewing them, you get to re-live the pain over and over again. You exaggerate the permanency of these issues by making sweeping generalizations, using words like "always" and "never". Since your subconscious can't take a joke, even if you've had a long period of time since the dreadful event you will reinforce the negative feelings you experienced. The pain seems here to stay indefinitely.

2. **Positive PAST Focus.** You say "I USED TO smoke (but I don't anymore), UP UNTIL NOW I would struggle with eating healthfully (but now I love the taste of healthy food), before today I had struggled with success in my sales

career (before my big close today), etc." You give acknowledgement to the past, not denying its reality, but recognizing that your past does not determine your future. Things can always be improved and you have the mindset and determination to do so.

3. **Negative PRESENT Focus.** Constant belittling of yourself, focusing solely on what you've done wrong. Most people slam themselves into a self-generated wall of internal negativity every day. You say "I'm so clumsy, I'm so forgetful, I'm so disorganized, I am a failure, I'm no good, no one likes me, I'm a screw-up, and I'm a loser." The words 'I am' are very powerful words and your mind will believe whatever you tell it. You are discounting all of the good qualities that are part of you and keeping only the worst. In fact, you may be exaggerating the worst.

4. **Positive Present Focus.** You use positive, present-tense affirmations like "I am a winner. I accomplish everything I set my mind to. I am a goal-achieving champion. I am the best at closing the sale." Some people might consider it unrealistically positive to say such things and argue that we are discounting the negative to do so. Perhaps, but if it works, who cares? Ultimately, if you can trick your mind into believing the best possible view of yourself and it makes you more effective, then the results speak for themselves. A very effective technique is to write out positive affirmations

for yourself and repeat them daily, like incantations. Remember that words without action will not yield results; you must follow through on your plans to accomplish your goal. Affirmations simply give you the mindset to perform more effectively.

5. **Negative Future Focus.** Mark Twain "I've faced many terrible things in life, some of which actually happened." This is the domain of worry and anxiety. "I'm going to fail, this won't work, I'm sure they'll be upset, the worst will happen," etc. Utterly crippling self talk that destroys dreams and lives. In almost every imaginable circumstance, this line of thinking is not only futile but destructive. Equally destructive is the phrase "I should". When you say "I should apply for that job" or "I should ask that girl out", the rest of the sentence is left unsaid. If you force yourself to complete the sentence out loud, you will quickly realize how insidious a silent negative thought can be. Expand "I should apply for that job"... why don't you? When you challenge yourself to answer the question, you might respond by saying "I should apply for the job... but I don't think I'm good enough". The negative poison is revealed. Saying "I should" usually makes people feel ashamed and guilty, not motivated; they feel they aren't living up to their potential.

6. **Positive Future Focus.** Fear and faith both make use of your imagination to conjure a vision of your future. The difference is that fear

imagines the worst possible ending, and faith imagines the best. It is your job to consciously choose to imagine the most desirable outcome; doing this will inspire the confidence to take action and help manifest your vision into reality. If you have failed in the past, say "NEXT TIME, I will get it right." This supports a positive future view. Another powerful way of representing the future is to state the goal you wish to achieve in present-tense, as if you have already accomplished it. "I am going to win the bodybuilding contest" or "I have closed the deal" when these events have not yet transpired is a very advanced and clever way to trick your subconscious into believing the new reality. When this happens, it helps give you the confidence to make that goal a reality.

	PAST-Tense	**PRESENT-Tense**	**FUTURE-Tense**
NEGATIVE Focus	I've never been good at that, I've always screwed up, I failed	I can't, I am: clumsy, forgetful, a failure	I will fail
POSITIVE Focus	I used to smoke/fail/cheat but I don't anymore; I've done it before, Look what I've accomplished successfully in the past!	I am: a winner, I have won the sale (stating the future in present tense as if you've accomplished the goal already!)	I can always accomplish what I set my mind to; if other men have done it, it's possible I can, NEXT TIME I will do better!

ACTION STEPS

1. **Decide to have a positive attitude!** Your attitude is a choice and you will reap what you sow. Other people don't choose your attitude; neither does the weather, the lineup at the bank or the traffic jam. YOU are in control, so make the adult decision to life your life with a more positive outlook!
2. **Ask positive questions.** Whenever you are faced with a tough situation, always fall back on "What's positive about this?" With practice, you will develop a toolbox of answers to draw on at a moments notice, and you will become more experienced and creative at finding your own answers to new situations.

3. **Listen to positive and motivational CD's.** The old computer programmer's credo of "Garbage in, garbage out" also applies to our minds. We must choose to stop listening to the trash news that only shows the negative and horrible things in the world, and ensure that we get a steady balance of good information to counteract the bad. Subscribe to a motivational information program and listen to cd's while you drive. My favorite cd's are from Tony Robbins, but there are many excellent speakers out there. For leadership wisdom cd's, I strongly recommend Orrin Woodward and Chris Brady, authors of the New York Times

Bestseller "Launching a Leadership Revolution".

4. **Associate with positive people**! Steel sharpens steel, and a rotten apple spoils the bunch. If you've got negative people hanging around you, make no mistake: their beliefs will infiltrate your own thought processes and you will start to think and act like they do. Because we are influenced by our peers, you must choose your peers wisely. This includes hanging around negative family members, neighbors and co-workers. If someone is verbally abusive to you and constantly puts you down, get rid of them, plain and simple. All quality relationships are built on respect. Secondly, if you hang around someone who is constantly whining, complaining, pointing out what is wrong, and just generally has a negative attitude, move on and find a better quality friend with whom you associate. When you hang around positive people, you feel a sense of possibility, opportunity, and courage in the face of doubt. Positive people believe things can be accomplished! You'll like yourself better, because you'll hear more positive feedback about what you are doing right. You'll see the good in people, because positive people see the good in you. Life is better being around positive winners!

CHAPTER 2:

TAKE THIS STRESS AND LOVE IT!

"If you are distressed by anything external, the pain is not due to the thing itself but to your own estimate of it; and this you have the power to revoke at any moment."
- Marcus Aurelius

It seems that no matter where I speak, the #1 topic that is requested of me is "how do I manage my stress?" Whether a person is working on the assembly line or in the C-Suite, stress seems to be an overwhelming part of our daily lives. Personally, my belief is that most of the stress that we experience is largely exaggerated and we initiate many of the situations that cause us stress. This assertion often frustrates people, but I would suggest that both of these points are exciting, because we have immediate and personal control over how we look at things, and how we react to them. However, time and time again I see grown adults *choose* not to handle stress well. Allow me to explain.

You can place two people in the same situation, and they can exhibit two totally different responses.

Have you ever seen two people in the same situation, and they exhibit two totally different responses? Perhaps they work for the same manager, or they are both in line at the grocery store, or in a traffic jam. One person remains calm and in control of themselves, and the second person has an absolute meltdown. What is the difference?

Consider a traffic jam. You're probably familiar with the term 'road rage'. This is the reaction that a small number of people have when they fly into a fit of anger due to something that occurs while driving (such as another driver cuts them off). If 100 people are in a traffic jam and experience bad behaviour from another driver, how many do you suppose get angry enough to experience road rage? The actual numbers vary depending upon your definition. However, a study of 111 Canadian drivers in 1998, found that:

- 27% made insulting gestures
- 21% deliberately cut off another driver
- 22% chased another car
- 7% have used the car as a weapon to attack
- 5% have gotten into a physical fight over driving[1]

So, what do you imagine may cause of their anger? If you were to ask them, they would say "The guy in the traffic jam made me angry". But if that were true, *everyone* around that guy in a traffic jam would experience road rage… and the fact is that they just *don't*. Since only a small percentage of people get angry, then the bad behaviour of a few individuals in a traffic jam cannot be the cause of their upset! It must be something else.

The variable in the equation is the person who gets angry: they cause themselves to get angry, because of their perception, their personality, their value system, the words they say to themselves in their head. So if stress is NOT the bad driver in the traffic jam, the line-up at the grocery store, or any external event… then what is it?

---

[1] Sheremata, D 1998, 'Road rage in the frozen north: A U.S. prof says Canadian drivers are more violent than Americans', *Alberta Report*, vol. 25, no. 27, pp. 32.

What Is Stress?

Stress is not the event that happens in front of us, or the person who exhibits a behaviour in our presence that we find "irritating"... stress is our *reaction* to those things. **Stress is our emotional and physiological response to any perceived threat, whether real or imagined**. The most important word in that definition is the word *perceived,* because the event doesn't even need to be real in order for you to experience stress. It could be a scary nightmare, an overwhelming phobia or a drug-induced hallucination.

My wife and I had an interesting experience in the building we lived in a few years ago: the elevator got stuck between two floors. It was my wife, myself and a third women trapped in the elevator for a few moments. The elevator doors started opening and closing against the concrete wall, and we were literally looking at the divider between the two floors. The elevator started jerking up and down, trying to get unstuck. After a few moments, my wife said "Give me your cell phone; I'm calling the building management to fix this because we've got to get going!" I had a different perspective. I was looking at the escape hatch in the roof of the elevator thinking *"Mission: Impossible! This is my chance to get to climb out of here like James Bond!"* I thought it was all very exciting and fun. However, the third person in the elevator, the woman beside me, did not find it exciting or fun. In fact, she was absolutely terrified. She was hyperventilating and on the verge of tears.

> ***Stress is our emotional and physiological response to any* perceived *threat, whether real or imagined.***
> -CJ Calvert

Why? Because she suffered from claustrophobia, which is a fear of confined spaces. She perceived that she was in danger being stuck in the elevator, and she reacted as if the threat was very real and very intense.

It is an interesting reminder, that all 3 of us were in the identical situation and had absolutely different reactions. But, is it possible for one person to react differently in the same situation from one moment to the next? Absolutely! The same event that doesn't bother you today might seem incredibly frustrating the next day, or even the next minute. All sorts of factors come into play: whether you've eaten lately or if you are hungry; if you didn't sleep and are fighting fatigue; if you are under the weather and combating illness; if you've been up all night with a new baby; if your alarm clock didn't wake you up in time and now you are late for work; if you spill a coffee in your lap; if the photocopier jams just when you are rushing to print something; if a customer or colleague chastises you for a mistake, or any number of other factors.

It might just seem like you are walking around with a cloud over your head and everything seems to be going wrong today. You might describe this as "getting up on the wrong side of the bed". It might seem like the day is just snowballing completely out of control: first the sleepless night, then you're late getting up, now the coffee, the client yells at you… and by the time the photocopier jams, you feel like you are on the verge of snapping! But let's keep this in perspective: a photocopier jamming is not really a big deal. However if you're looking at the situation in the context of a day where it is the tenth thing in a row to go wrong, you start to be so sensitive to any upset that the smallest irritant can be magnified in your mind to be completely distorted and seem much larger than it is in reality.

Climbing Big Chief

I faced an interesting situation managing my "stress response" in the summer of 2004 when I was mountain climbing in British Columbia. I was climbing up a part of Big Chief in Squamish (a renowned mountain in an area known for incredible climbing) and my climbing guide Geoff and I were doing what is called "crack climbing". What this is can best be described this way: picture a flat sheet of rock that goes hundreds of feet in the air, but the rock has a straight vertical crack right up the middle. The crack in some places is big enough to slide your entire arm in and is a foot wide; in other places it's less than half an inch wide and you can barely manage to slide the tips of your fingers into it. Wedging our fingers and our toes into the crack, this is what we were using to climb up the side of the mountain. (And yes, I actually paid to have my guide take me up this part of the mountain!)

Now, Geoff was lead climbing. Climbers move in partnership, where one person lead climbs and sets the course; this means that they climb up with the rope attached to their waist harness and it dangles down below them. Every 10 feet or so, the lead climber pauses and with one hand, takes a clip off of his belt (called a carabiner), forces it into the crack and attaches his rope to it. The lead climber continues this way up the face of the mountain. If he falls, he'll only fall a maximum of 20 feet (and will bounce, hopefully gently, off of the rock face). The job of the guy at the bottom (which was me) is to feed rope out at the same pace as the guide was climbing; no more and no less. Too slow and I might cause him to fall; too much and if he slips he could fall much more than necessary. Once Geoff climbed about 50 feet, he would create a temporary camp and lock himself onto the rock face using 3-5 carabiner clips. This is all very safe if you do it correctly (which, of course, is the trick!). Once Geoff was secure, I would release all of my clips from the rock face, re-attach them to my belt and begin ascending. Each time I reached one of the clips that Geoff had left in the rock, I would pause to unclip my rope from it, dislodge it from the rock and attach it to my belt.

Well, we were having an absolutely awesome day. The weather couldn't have been better, there were no other climbers on our rock face so we weren't tripping over them or slowing them down (like you might experience on a golf course when other people are playing at a different pace than you) and the scenery was absolutely breathtaking. I paused to soak in the beauty of the view: 400 feet in the air, mountains in all direction, and the canopy of the treetops hundreds of feet beneath us. Wow! What an adventure. I pulled out my camera and got a few great photos. This was so exciting! I was hundreds of feet in the air, hanging by a rope! I was having so much fun.

Then something interesting happened. It suddenly occurred to me *"Holy #$@! I'm hundreds of feet in the air, hanging by a rope!"* Instantly, I was no longer feeling "excited". I was feeling "terrified". My heart rate accelerated, my breathing became labored, and I started to freak out. There was no one to call for help, there was no "time out", there was no way to climb down. I couldn't communicate with Geoff, since you cannot hear each other when you are that high due to the noise of the wind. Geoff could not risk his life to detach and climb down. It was completely up to me. I started pouring sweat. All I could picture was the dizzying height, the sheer rock face, and the life-threatening danger of the situation that I had deliberately volunteered to do for fun!

I gripped the rock for dear life, hanging on the rope, closed my eyes, hummed desperately, sang songs, talked out loud to myself… anything I could think to do in the moment to distract myself and calm down. I forced myself to look up, focus on Geoff, and start climbing again. Going up and finishing the climb was the only option to get out of the situation safely.

Now, here is my question to you: at first, I was having a lot of fun. I was enjoying the excitement, the adventure, the breathtaking view at 400 feet. Then a moment later, I was absolutely panicking. So what happened to change my emotional state? Did the rope start to fray? Did the buckles on my harness start to come undone? Did the straps on my harness start to break? NO. In fact, absolutely nothing happened physically. But something must have changed, because one moment I was happy and then the next moment I was terrified. Something did change. My PERCEPTION changed. As long as I viewed the situation as fun and exciting, that is what I felt. The moment I viewed the situation as a threat, I reacted as if the threat were real.

Most Fears Are Learned

"There is great beauty in going through life without anxiety or fear. Half our fears are baseless, and the other half discreditable."
- John Christian Boyee

"The only thing we have to fear is fear itself."
- Franklin D. Roosevelt

Most of the time when we get stressed, we are not in physical danger. The danger we fear is almost always a figment of our imagination. Babies are born with only two natural fears: the fear of loud noises, and the fear of falling. Thus, anything else that you fear is a *learned* fear.

Let me give you a very common example: public speaking. The technical term for this fear is glossophobia. I've heard a statistic which states that speaking in front of an audience is the #1 fear for most people. Isn't that amazing! (I guess I'm strange in that I get excited by the size of the audience; give me 5000 people for a few hours and I'm in Heaven! But I clearly recognize that this would be terrifying for most people.)

Consider what happens for a person mentally, physically and emotionally when they start to get scared. What sort of words are they saying to themselves? Are they saying *"Wow! I'm an incredible speaker! These people look so happy to see me!"*, or do you think they might be saying something else? Without question, they are saying things like *"I'm going to screw up, I'm going to forget what I was supposed to say, my PowerPoint will crash, I'll make a fool of myself, everyone is staring at me, I feel so embarrassed, and this is going to be terrible!"*

When a person starts saying these things to themselves, what do you suppose starts to happen to their heart rate? It increases. What about their rate of breath? Are they breathing slow, relaxed, deep breaths? No; their breathing is rapid and shallow. In fact, they might even be holding their breath. What about their hands; are they calm and steady? No; their hands are shaking along with their knees, because all of the adrenaline coursing through their body is making them shake. What about their digestive tract? Is their tummy nice and relaxed? No, it feels like their stomach is doing somersaults. The nickname for this queasy feeling is "butterflies in your stomach". This feeling is occurring because blood is being diverted away from their digestive tract. These reactions, along with a host of others, are all the same reactions that occur in times of extreme stress when you believe you are in mortal danger. However, when you are speaking, you aren't in mortal danger. *(Unless you're really bad!)* However, you might believe that you are in social danger, fearing that you will be ostracized, laughed at, singled out, made fun of, etc.

The human mind does not distinguish between something that is actually happening versus something that is vividly imagined.

This raises a critical point as to why people are so stressed: the human mind does not distinguish between something that is actually happening versus something that is vividly imagined. That's how you can have a scary, violent nightmare and wake up with the sheets soaked with sweat and your heart is racing. As far as your brain is concerned, the scary images in your imagination may as well be real, since they *seemed* real enough. Once the "launch sequence" is initiated in your fight-or-flight response, it is very difficult to interrupt.

Only React When The Threat Is Real

"Men often bear little grievances with less courage than they do large misfortunes."
- Aesop

The only time we should really get stressed in when we are in actual physical danger. I had a situation a couple of months ago where, while driving in my car on the highway, a trailer truck decided to come to a dead stop in front of me. And by dead stop, I mean that he was doing 120km/hr one moment, and the next moment he slammed on his breaks and was no longer moving forward; he was doing ZERO km/hr. The reason? The lane we were in was coming to an end because of construction on the highway, and they had set up a series of orange pylons to guide people into changing lanes. However, for some reason this guy didn't change lanes, he just flat stopped.

Well, the next few seconds seemed like they moved in slow-motion. I went to crank my wheel to the left and swerve around the guy, but just as I was doing this another car was passing through my blind spot beside me. I slammed on my brakes as hard as I could, literally lifting off my seat and STANDING on the brakes. Immediately, I heard the horrible screeching sound of my tires as I tried desperately to come to a dead stop on the highway. The cabin of my car was instantly filled with the acrid smoke of burning rubber as the treads were seared off of my tires. There was no thought as to whether or not someone was behind me, because I was about to drive right through this truck.

I watched in slow-motion as I slid right towards the back of the truck, and I had one final split-second to think the thought "I'm going to hit him". I cranked my wheel to the right, smashed through the construction pylons and slid to a stop in a spray of gravel. If any construction worker had been standing there on the shoulder, he would have been flattened.

Well, the guy in the truck takes a look around, sees that everything in his world is just peachy, and drives off! I do not, however, just drive off. In fact, I didn't move for about 10 minutes. It took about that amount of time to slow my heart, because my heart was pounding so hard I thought it was going to jump out of my chest. My hands were shaking, and I could barely dial my wife to say "I love you" and ask to hear my baby son on the phone. I needed some comfort and validation that I had actually made it through the moment!

The point is that it's absolutely acceptable and expected that you get stressed out if you're in physical danger. But most people react the same way to everything that might bother them, and most things we react to are just plain silly! In the long run, this just isn't a healthy way of going through life! We've got to learn some strategies to calm ourselves down.

It's Actually Good To Have Some Stress

"It is not in the still calm of life, or the repose of a pacific station, that great characters are formed.... Great necessities call out great virtues."
- Abigail Adams

Contrary to popular believe, it's actually a good idea to have a *little* bit of stress in life. The opposite of stress is boredom. Without any pressures, any deadlines, anything challenging us to perform, we will just slack off and lay around the poolside, sipping margaritas and playing yet another round of golf before we get our afternoon massage. (You might be thinking "that doesn't sound so bad!")

Of course, it *sounds* great! In fact, it's great for about a week; maximum two weeks. But after that short time, you start getting restless. You may have heard of this experience; it's called "cabin fever". People are *not* meant to be terminally lazy and directionless. We are goal-achieving animals and we don't do well to have eons of unstructured time. (This is one of the reasons why retirement can be such a challenge for people who were highly productive on the job, and then don't have a full schedule of activities planned for their newfound time off.) It can start to feel very unpleasant just sitting around doing nothing.

When we have just the right amount of stress, we are motivated to push ourselves beyond our normal limits and achieve extraordinary results. I'm sure we've all had days where the stakes were high, the chips were down and somehow we miraculously managed to accomplish what seemed almost impossible at the time. And isn't it true that when we pull off a seemingly miraculous accomplishment, we feel absolutely incredible! That sort of pride in beating the odds can make you feel invincible, and you get to spend the rest of the day walking around like you are ten feet tall. This is the moment where stress in an incalculable asset: with just enough pressure, your true genius is revealed.

Stress becomes a problem when we tip past the point of stress being a benefit, and instead of looking at a problem as a challenge to be overcome we view it as an insurmountable obstacle that will crush us. Whether real or imagined, if you don't think you can handle the problem you face, if you think that it is too big, coming at you too fast, or that you don't have the skills and experience to pull off a victory, you're going to get stressed and go into what scientists refer to as the "fight-or-flight" response.

> *With just enough pressure, your true genius is revealed.*
> -CJ Calvert

WHAT IS THE "FIGHT-OR-FLIGHT" RESPONSE?

The fight-or-flight response (otherwise known as the stress response) is our rapid physiological response to a mortal threat, for example at the hands of a predator. To quickly summarize, this response gives you an immediate surge of energy that allows you either to run for your life away from the predator (flight) or if you cannot run fast enough, to turn and defend yourself even if it is a fight to the death (fight).

Scientists also show that there is a third option, "freeze", where an animal will become paralyzed when encountering a predator in an instinctual effort to remain unseen. This can be seen in the well-intended but ill-advised tendency of animals to freeze on the highway when caught in the headlights of automobiles. For the simplicity of our discussion we will choose to focus on fight and flight.

Let's suppose you are in a situation where you perceive a mortal threat: you are camping in the woods and you run into a bear. This is generally regarded as a threatening situation to life and limb! Here is what happens:

- **Stage 1: The Event Occurs**. Whatever the threatening event is, whether it is running into a bear in the woods, almost colliding with a van on the highway, or for any men reading this book… if your wife wants to talk about "feelings". This can be pretty scary for some guys. ☺

- **Stage 2: Your Evaluation**. This is where you decided whether or not the event is worth getting stressed out over. You soak in all of the data from the situation through your five senses: visual (sight), auditory (sound), kinesthetic (touch), olfactory (smell) and gustatory (taste/digestion). You consider all of the millions of bits of data within a split second to decide whether or not this situation is dangerous. If you decide it is, you are going to get stressed. However, if you DON'T think it is worth getting stressed over, you just simply aren't going to get stressed. Your evaluation literally has the power to make-or-break your stress response on the spot. If you are walking down the highway and you are about to be run down buy a truck, but you don't hear or see it coming, you aren't going to get stressed, even though you are in mortal danger. If you are absolutely drunk, you could be in the woods and the bear could be standing over you licking your face… and you still aren't going to get stressed if you've passed out! You might be lying there dreaming that you're at the spa and you're getting a steaming hot towel on your face. However, if you decide you ARE in danger, you go to the next stage…

- **Stage 3: Chemical Response**. Once you've decided you're in danger, your hypothalamus recruits the sympathetic nervous system. A signal is sent to your adrenaline glands to begin producing adrenaline, cortisol & cortisone[2]. These in turn create a cascade of physiological reactions

- **Stage 4: Physiological Reaction**. In response to the chemicals flooding your body, your body gears up so that you can either run for your life,

[2] http://en.wikipedia.org/wiki/Cortisone

or fight to the death. Some of the reactions commonly associated with this fight-or-flight response include:

- Increased heart rate and blood pressure to make blood delivery more efficient
- Diversion of blood from less essential systems (like digestion) to most life-saving essential systems
- Shortness of breath from rapid, shallow breathing
- Heightened sense of sight and hearing
- Increased energy by releasing glucose stores
- Surge of endorphins to block pain signals from any injury sustained in the fight
- The release of cortisol also limits or stops activity in other less-essential systems like the immune system or the reproductive system
- Your liver begins releasing additional energy stores (such as fat and cholesterol)

What Are The Consequences?

"You don't get ulcers from what you eat. You get them from what's eating you."
- Vicki Baum

If you don't learn to manage your stress, do you believe that eventually your health will suffer? Absolutely! In fact, the pioneering father of stress research, Montreal doctor Hans Selye, says that

"Mental tensions, frustrations, insecurity, aimlessness are among the most damaging stressors, and psychosomatic studies have shown how often they cause migraine headache, peptic ulcers, heart attacks, hypertension, mental disease, suicide, or just hopeless unhappiness." Here are some of the potential consequences of unmanaged stress, from the mundane to the life-threatening:

- Fatigue
- Irritability
- Muscle tension, particularly in our neck, shoulders and back
- Lack of concentration
- Forgetfulness
- Gastro-intestinal challenges including stomach upset, diarrhea, and ulcers
- Compromised immune system
- Cardiovascular challenges, including increased blood pressure or hypertension
- Heart attack
- Stroke

With all of the possible negative consequences, it is vital that we take positive action to mitigate the stressors we face in our daily lives and enjoy a more relaxed, enjoyable day!

What Are Your Triggers?

"The size of a man can be determined by the size of the thing it takes to anger him."
- Unknown source, as quoted by Kevin Kooger

Since people can respond differently to the same situation, it's valuable to identify the things that you know will cause you to feel frustrated. I've provided a checklist below of behaviours or situations that might "stress you out". Knowing your triggers allows you to develop coping strategies in advance; it also allows you to communicate to the people around you what your sensitivities are so that they can minimize any innocent missteps.

Behaviours. When other people:

- ❑ speak loudly on their cell phone
- ❑ cut you off in the middle of speaking
- ❑ finish your sentences for you
- ❑ use profanity
- ❑ use insulting or hurtful remarks
- ❑ are upset with you, but won't admit to it when asked
- ❑ use passive/aggressive behaviour to sabotage you instead of dealing with a problem directly
- ❑ invade your personal space
- ❑ make threatening gestures
- ❑ raise their voice
- ❑ over-commit and under-deliver
- ❑ act like a doormat and accept bad behaviour
- ❑ can't make a decision

- ❑ lie
- ❑ cheat
- ❑ betray your trust
- ❑ break your confidence and share your secrets with others
- ❑ blame you for their mistakes
- ❑ take credit for your accomplishments
- ❑ always hog all of the attention
- ❑ are totally irresponsible
- ❑ are disorganized and lose everything
- ❑ are chronically late for meetings and appointments
- ❑ are thoughtless and devoid of empathy
- ❑ are selfish or greedy
- ❑ are obnoxiously competitive
- ❑ are compulsive perfectionists
- ❑ don't return phone calls or emails
- ❑ won't answer questions directly
- ❑ won't keep their promises
- ❑ don't signal when changing lanes
- ❑ cut you off while changing lanes
- ❑ speed while driving
- ❑ OTHER: ____________________

Situations:

- ❑ caught in traffic
- ❑ stuck in a lineup at the grocery store
- ❑ the alarm clock doesn't go off
- ❑ buying a new home and moving in
- ❑ arranging a wedding ceremony
- ❑ sleepless nights with a new baby

- ❑ technology problems: the PowerPoint won't work, etc, our computer hard drive crashes, our spam folder accidentally catches and deletes an important email
- ❑ We are fighting physical discomfort, illness, fatigue, migraine headaches, stomach upset
- ❑ OTHER: ____________________

We cause ourselves stress by:

- ❑ procrastination
- ❑ disorganization
- ❑ losing important documents
- ❑ can't find our car keys
- ❑ cell phone isn't charged
- ❑ not saving for "rainy day" emergencies
- ❑ not planning meals ahead of time so we eat junk food, or we eat nothing at all
- ❑ haven't confirmed hotel reservations
- ❑ running out of gasoline, not checking our tires, or not changing our oil
- ❑ not taking care of our health through poor diet, lack of exercise, not getting a check-up with our doctor
- ❑ ignoring our most valuable relationships
- ❑ snapping in frustration at the people we love
- ❑ OTHER: ____________________

STRATEGIES FOR REDUCING STRESS

Now that we've discussed the 4 stages of the fight-or-flight response, we can use that understanding to design some powerful strategies to mitigate our stress. Let's literally go down the list, from stage 1 to stage 4, and create strategies to literally stop our stress in its tracks!

Stage 1: Stop The Event From Happening

"What man's mind can create, man's character can control."
- Thomas A. Edison

It just makes sense that if you know what triggers your stress, if you can avoid the trigger then you will avoid the stress. For example, if traffic jams tend to frustrate you, then if you listen to the news or look at the internet highway traffic cameras, you can pinpoint where the accident is and drive around it. The result: you avoid the trigger of your stress, so you avoid the stress itself!

What you want to do is ask yourself "Is there any way that I can control this event from happening?" If it is possible to prevent it from happening, stop it quickly if it has happened or minimize its impact, then you will manage the stress quite well. Consider the stress of having a fire potentially break out on your stove. The three steps to managing this from creating stress are Prevent, Stop and Minimize.

Prevent: Don't put anything flammable near the stove, and don't leave the stove unattended while on. This will prevent a fire.

Stop: If a fire starts, you could have planned ahead and had a fire extinguisher next to the stove to stop the fire from spreading and getting any worse if it does start.

Minimize: If you can't stop the fire, you can minimize the total damage inflicted (and total stress created!) by having enough fire insurance to pay for any damage. You can also ensure your family's safety by installing smoke alarms in the house with new batteries, practice fire drills and develop escape plans for your family including rope ladders out of upstairs windows

Think about how you might apply this to a situation that consistently frustrates you. What you want to do is look for patterns; if something happens once a week, and has happened every week for the last couple of months, there is a good chance it is going to happen again this week and you're going to get frustrated. For example, suppose your manager comes to you Friday at 4:59 each week and says "I'm so sorry, I just need you to finish this up before you leave," and they hand you an hour of paperwork to be completed. That might be frustrating! But if they do it all the time, you can expect it and try to find a solution. Perhaps you could set an email reminder to yourself for 4:00 to go to their desk and ask them if they have any work that needs to be completed by 5:00, since you'll be leaving at that time to pick up your kids promptly from day care. There's a good chance they've had the work sitting on their desk all day and they've simply forgotten to pass it onto you! One simple action on your part and the stressful situation is averted.

Stage #2: Control Your Perspective

"The strong man is the one who is able to intercept at will the communication between the senses and the mind."
- Napoleon Bonaparte

If you can't stop or control the situation that causes you stress (Stage #1), your next option is to control your evaluation (Stage #2). Whatever your perspective, if you think something is worth getting stressed out over it, you're going to get stressed. The simple solution at this point is to remember that your perspective or "attitude" has massive control over your stress response. Remember that a person can be paralyzed with fear because of an intense phobia like claustrophobia in an elevator, whereas other people remain totally calm. Your positive perspective can either throw proverbial water on the fire of your stress, or your negative perspective can throw gasoline on the fire. If you choose to perceive something as a threat, your body will respond as if it actually were. We've already discussed this at length in the previous chapter on positive attitude, so take action and implement all of the tools that I've shared the next time you face a situation that challenges your patience. These are the tools that I personally use!

I had a situation where I was driving my trusty Toyota Tercel down the highway near my home in Toronto in April of 2006. Toyota's are absolutely fantastic; you could call me a "raving fan" to use Ken Blanchard's term. The car was just amazing. After 7 years of driving the car 1000 kilometers a week, I had logged 346,000 km on the odometer. In this period of time, I never had to do a single thing to fix the engine! In fact, the only thing that I ever repaired or replaced was the oil, the tires and the brakes. The engine was amazing. The engine was indestructible. And that morning, my engine… *exploded*! And I don't mean that it "broke" or it "stopped"… I mean it blew up while I was driving!

Well, I got the car to the side of the road with blue smoke pouring out from under the hood. When I popped the hood, the engine was sputtering, hissing, with what looked like little bits of metal and rubber all over the engine block. It was a mess! Here I was, dressed in a suit on my way to deliver a presentation and my car was toast. So I asked myself what any self-respecting positive-attitude speaker might ask in such a situation:

"What's so positive about *this!?!?*"

Well, it took me a few moments to come up with an answer. At first I thought "Well, at least no one was hurt." Then I thought about it: I'm driving a 7-year old car and the engine just exploded. Do you know what's positive about that?

I get a brand new car! *That's* what's positive!

Stage #3: Manage Your Chemical Intake

If you can't stop the event from happening, and if you can't keep a positive attitude, your body sends a signal to your adrenal gland and you go into the third stage: your chemical response. While it is unlikely that you will have conscious control over the production of these chemicals, we must also recognize that any chemicals we introduce in our body can soothe or exacerbate our stress response. (The strategies that I'm sharing here are all related to managing the chemicals in our body, although admittedly I'm going to be describing chemicals other that adrenaline and cortisol. Just for simplicity I've decided to group all of these concepts together and describe them in this section.)

Some people then turn to chemicals to manage their stress levels. This is rarely a good idea, most particularly if you are the one administering the chemicals. One of the most common ways of altering you moods is by drinking alcohol. I don't ever suggest drinking to manage anxiety or depression. (For the record, I don't like the bitter taste of beer and wine and never drink it. I also don't like the dizzy experience of intoxication, so I just don't do it.) There is nothing wrong with having a glass of wine or a bottle of beer, but please use moderation with alcohol. I also don't agree with using illegal drugs. It's obvious, though, that many people use drugs and alcohol to lift their spirits or drown their sorrows.

In cases like depression or overwhelming anxiety, I would recommend that you consult a psychiatrist, or at the very least your family doctor. If a psychiatrist prescribes anti-depressant medication, by all means follow the prescription. But please don't alter the prescription and think "I know the doctor said only take one pill a day, but today is Monday and I've had a really bad time at work... I'm going to take 5 pills!" That is a profoundly *bad idea*. Always follow the directions of a psychiatrist in these cases.

There is one final way of ingesting chemicals to manage your mood. It is very popular, much less insidious, and completely legal. It is called eating "comfort food". You've probably heard this term. The reason for the name is that the food tends to comfort people. Food never cheats on you, never lets you down, it's always there at 2am when you're feeling down, and it won't talk about you behind your back. It's like a trusted and loyal friend for many people. The most popular form of comfort food seems to be chocolate! My own personal experience suggests that women tend to eat chocolate to lift their spirits more than men do. Do you know why? Because it works!

When you ingest chocolate, it causes a release of a neurotransmitter called endorphins. Endorphins have the same chemical structure as morphine, yet they are 100 times more powerful. They block the pain signal from reaching the brain during times of high stress, so that if you are injured in a fight you literally will not feel it until after the fight is done. But a massive dose of endorphins causes you to feel euphoric... you just simply feel happy! Chocolate can help with this, which is one reason for its popularity (along with the fact it tastes great). But again, all things in moderation: don't go eating slabs of chocolate when you're depressed. Overeating obviously leads to obesity and a host of related health challenges.

In conclusion, there is rarely a good chemical-related stress management strategy that I'm going to recommend (unless prescribed by a psychiatrist). So if you don't drink the problem away, what's left to manage your stress?

Stage #4: Change Your Physiology

"For fast-acting relief try slowing down."
- Lily Tomlin

And finally, if you can't stop the situation (Stage #1), you can't look at it positively (Stage #2), you wisely choose not to drink the problem away (Stage #3), you are now in full-fledged fight-or-flight response. Your heart rate has dramatically accelerated, your breathing is rapid and shallow, your digestive system is shutting down and adrenaline is coursing through your body. You are sitting at your desk, driving your car, or sitting at your kitchen table, and you are stressed out. So, now what? Because the stress reaction is a PHYSICAL REACTION in your body, it demands a physiological intervention in order to calm yourself down at this point. So what's the best way to calm down your body? The top three interventions I recommend at this stage are Exercise, Laughter and Deep Breathing.

- **Exercise**. Please remember that during the fight-or-flight response, your body wants to either run, or fight. Your heart is pounding, your hands are shaking with adrenaline… your body is primed for action. However, I would not recommend "running" in most situations, particularly if you are at work. It does nothing positive for your career if you run screaming from the building with your hair on fire. Clearly, this will limit your future promotability. I also don't recommend "fighting", even when at the office. As much as you might want to reach across the boardroom table and "adjust someone's tie", don't do it! Firstly, it's illegal, and secondly, you still won't get promoted. However, your body is fueled and ready to charge. So what do you do? You go home and exercise! Exercise is a fantastic way of burning off the stress response and returning you to homeostasis (the body's normal state of stress-free calm). So go home and exercise! Just remember to do intense exercise in order to mimic the intensity of running or fighting; light or moderate exercise may not be sufficient. Besides, after 20 minutes of brutally intense exercise, you're not going to be feeling any stress… you'll just feel *pain!* Obviously, it's easier to do this at home rather than at work. You can't really turn to a colleague in a meeting and say "You know, you are really ticking me off… so I'm going to do some pushups! And, when I'm done, we'll keep talking!"

- **Laughter**. For the same reason as chocolate, laughter is an excellent stress-reliever because it causes a surge of endorphins. Most people have figured out that laughter makes them feel good, even if they don't understand the chemistry behind it. They just know that if they go home and watch their favorite sit-com on television like "Friends" or "Seinfeld" they'll feel better. So, since you now understand this, why don't your purposely add more humour to your day. Read the comics, watch funny videos (just not when you're supposed to be working!), watch funny movies. One of my favorite things to do is listen to comedy CD's while I drive my car in traffic. I already know that I'm going to get stuck in traffic occasionally; why wouldn't I try to find a way to enjoy it more? You end up laughing all the way to work and all the way back home, and you get to your destination in a great mood! (Besides, the people in front of you in the traffic jam see that you in their rear-view mirror laughing like a madman, they think you're crazy, and they just simply move out of the way and let you through!)

- **Deep Breathing**. This is my #1 favorite stress-managing technique. It is the fastest, easiest, most appropriate tool in the most number of situations. The reason it works is because when we are in fight-or-flight mode, we start breathing rapid, shallow breaths. This gives a quick influx of oxygen. But then we hold our breath, particularly when we are exerting ourselves by sprinting or exerting our muscles in a fight. Think of any time you are exercising at the gym and lifting heavy weights, or you pick up something really heavy, or you sprint up a flight of stairs. The chances are that once you stop at the top of the stairs, you realize that you were holding your breath the entire time! Try it and you'll see what I'm talking about. Why do we do this? Because in fight-or-flight mode, our brain is making very quick decisions about where to spend energy and where to save it. All of us can hold our breath for a short period of time, because we are very inefficient with processing oxygen. When we breathe in air, it is 24% oxygen, and when we exhale, what we exhale still contains 16% oxygen. This is how we are able to do CPR and deliver some oxygen to our patient by blowing into their mouth. Since the average person can hold their breath for about 30 seconds, your brain decides during intense situations that for the next 30 seconds, you are simply going to skip breathing! The reason that deep breathing works is that you are taking conscious control over your body's stress reaction. Unless you are a Tibetan monk, you likely don't have conscious control over your heart rate or your adrenal glands, but everyone can choose to breathe more slowly. When you breathe slow, deep breathes in, pause, and slowly exhale, you put the brakes on your whole sympathetic nervous system and you calm yourself right down. The great thing is that you can use this strategy in almost every situation: while you are driving, at home or at your desk at work.

You can even do it while you are having a tense conversation: while the other person is talking, just pay attention to your rate of breath and calm your breathing down. The other person can't get mad at you for this; they aren't going to say *"Hey! Are you breathing?!?! No* breathing *while I'm* talking!"

The Secret Is Just To Remember

The point to all of these strategies is not that they are complicated, because they aren't. All of these strategies are common sense, and you probably knew about and agreed with most all of them. The issue isn't whether you know a good way to reduce stress; it's whether you can remember to use the strategy when you're stressed. That's when it's hard to remember! So, however you need to do it, you've got to figure out a way of reminding yourself to follow through on these strategies. Sometimes I will write a note to myself on the back of my business card and keep it in my pocket; every time I need it, it's right there to remind me. Maybe you put a Post-it note on your computer monitor. Whatever you do, pick a few key strategies and implement them when the pressure is on. If you do so, you're going to find that problems don't seem as big as they used to, your day gets easier, you start having more fun and life is simply more enjoyable on a daily basis!

50 TIPS TO REDUCE STRESS

What follows is a massive list of stress-reduction tips and tricks that I've amassed over the years. As you scan down the list, put a checkmark next to the tips that you think might be helpful and enjoyable for you!

- ❑ Count to ten
- ❑ Smile more often
- ❑ Eat nutritious food that energizes you
- ❑ Listen to your favorite music
- ❑ Play games with friends
- ❑ Share a joke with a friend
- ❑ Dress in a way that makes you feel good
- ❑ Wake up at the same time each day to avoid morning fatigue
- ❑ Talk to a trusted friend
- ❑ Stop and smell the roses
- ❑ Plan ahead
- ❑ If possible, avoid situations that cause you stress
- ❑ Ask "What's positive about this?"
- ❑ Read a good book
- ❑ Watch your favorite TV program
- ❑ Get some fresh air

- ❑ Change your focus
- ❑ Know your limits
- ❑ Play some games
- ❑ Enjoy your favorite hobby
- ❑ Avoid coffee, drink juice and water instead
- ❑ Don't blame yourself
- ❑ Ask for help
- ❑ Realize that "This too shall pass"
- ❑ Leave your work at the office
- ❑ Partake in a massage
- ❑ Enjoy a catnap
- ❑ Soak in a warm bubble bath
- ❑ Always, ALWAYS, take a lunch break
- ❑ Get some sleep
- ❑ Find the silver lining
- ❑ Plan your time
- ❑ Prioritize
- ❑ Get organized
- ❑ Be on time to meetings
- ❑ If you are worried, just prepare more
- ❑ When you're feeling down, volunteer and help someone else
- ❑ Don't avoid a problem and let it grow
- ❑ Clear your conscience
- ❑ Act with integrity
- ❑ Speak positively of others
- ❑ Notice what you do right and feel proud of yourself
- ❑ Dale Carnegie says "Don't condemn, complain or criticize"
- ❑ Admit your mistakes
- ❑ Deep breathing
- ❑ Intense Exercise
- ❑ Stretch

- ❑ Take a yoga or Pilates class
- ❑ Put on your favorite music, get up and dance!
- ❑ Squeeze a stress ball

ACTION STEPS

1. Identify the common triggers that get you flustered, ticked off, or angry.
2. Ask yourself: Is there anything I can do to prevent, stop or minimize these stressors?
3. Ask yourself: What is positive about this situation? Look for the silver lining, what's funny, or the good in every encounter
4. Exercise, laugh, engage in deep breathing… do whatever is necessary to calm your body down!

CHAPTER 3:

MAKE EVERY MOMENT COUNT

"We all sorely complain of the shortness of time, and yet have much more than we know what to do with. Our lives are either spent in doing nothing at all, or in doing nothing to the purpose, or in doing nothing that we ought to do. We are always complaining that our days are few, and acting as though there would be no end of them."
- Marcus Annaeus Seneca

In the realm of personal development, there is no single ability that will impact your life more than the ability to manage your time. It is one of the beauties of our life experience that there exists a level playing field that is fair and just and equal to all men. ***That playing field is time.*** It is thrilling to me that every human alive is given the same 24 hours to do with as they please.

Consider the equity in this, the arena of time. No matter what country you are born into, whether your parents are wealthy or not, connected or not, supportive or not, whether you have a degree of athletic prowess or intellectual ability, you are still gifted with the same 24 hours as every other person alive. No amount of favoritism can bless you with extra time; no amount of injustice can reduce your daily allotment. You cannot spend 23 hours today and bank an hour for a future date; nor can you say "Today I need 25 hours, and I'll draw against my future account."

> *The word "NOW" is a potent call-to-arms for men of action. The word "LATER" is the death-knell of the procrastinator.*
> **-CI Calvert**

But whether you are a president or a paper boy, you get the exact same amount. You have all the time that exists. What is different between people is that all successful people have mastered the art of wringing every bit of possibility from each fleeting moment. Upon closer examination, you would find that the champions of life realize that time is their most precious resource, because it is utterly irreplaceable. You can always earn more money, but you couldn't spend a billion dollars to purchase one extra minute of time.

Many people complain regularly that they do not have enough time. We mourn the lost opportunities of the past, daydream wistfully of the possibilities of the future, and yet we squander the only moment to which we have access. John Howe says *"What a folly it is to dread the thought of throwing away life at once, and yet have no regard to throwing it away by parcels and piecemeal."* It is a fallacy to believe that the current moment doesn't count. Yet this seems to be the belief of all common men. **The word "NOW" is a potent call-to-arms for men of action. The word "LATER" is the death-knell of the procrastinator.** It is up to you to decide which one you adopt as your battle cry.

What Is "Time Management"?

"Two things are as big as the man who possesses them, neither bigger nor smaller. One is a minute, the other is a dollar."
- Channing Pollock

The concept of time is simply a measuring tool to gauge the rate of motion between two moving objects that are either moving toward one another or moving apart. When people traditionally think of time management, they consider the various activities that they feel they would like to accomplish, they consider how much time it would reasonably take to accomplish them, and they try to follow this plan.

It might seem that the more successful time manager would be the one who moves the fastest. **On the contrary, the most effective time manager is the**

one who has the highest rate of return for the smallest unit of time invested. Thus, being the fastest at accomplishing the most number of tasks that yield a small unit of return is inconsequential when compared with the incalculable value of accomplishing a task with the highest ROI. The greatest time-management warrior doesn't get the most *number* of tasks accomplished; they get the most number of *high-value tasks* accomplished. They figure out a way to make their hour of work yield 10 times the profit over their previous performance.

> *You cannot "manage" time. You can only manage yourself within time.*
> -CJ Calvert

The phrase "time management" is a bit of a misnomer. **You cannot "manage" time. You can only manage yourself *within* time.** The phrase properly refers to a set of competencies that all effective people possess: the ability to understand what is important (**prioritization**), the ability the build your schedule around your priorities (**planning**), the ability to minimize distractions (**focus**) and the ability to execute your plan (**motivation vs. procrastination**). The ultimate difference between people who operate at maximum efficiency and the people who squander their time is in the decisions they make about what to do and when to do it.

PRIORITIZATION

The Story of the "Glass Jar"

Years ago, I heard a story that illustrated the concept of prioritization brilliantly. The story, from an unknown source and shared in Stephen Covey's book "First Things First", is as follows:

A professor walked into his MBA class carrying a large glass jar. The students could see that the jar was jam-packed with big rocks. The professor placed the heavy jar on his desk and turned to the class, smiling.

"Pop quiz on time-management", he said. "This jar is your schedule. The rocks in the jar are the events in your schedule, such as reports and projects. The question is: how much time do you have left?"

Well, the students were a bit surprised by this; after all, it was clearly obvious that the jar was so full, that not one more rock could be placed in the jar. They answered "We have no more time!"

The professor smiled. He reached under his desk and pulled out a pail filled with gravel. He poured the gravel into the top of the jar and the students watched as the gravel filled in all the space around the big rocks. The professor smiled a second time and asked "Okay, NOW how much time do you have?"

Well, the students were surprised. They hadn't considered that he would use gravel, but now all the space around the big rocks looked like it had been filled in. "There is no time left!" they cried.

The professor reached under his desk and pulled out a second pail, this time filled with sand. He slowly poured the sand into the top of the jar, pausing every so often to shake the jar and allow the sand to sift gently down and fill in all the remaining space around the gravel. "How much more time do you have?"

Now the students were really surprised. But it was clear by looking at the jar that all the remaining space had been filled in. "You have no more time!" they cried.

The professor reached under his desk a third and final time and pulled out a third pail filled with water. He poured the water into the top of the jar, and this time it did fill in all the remaining space. He put the empty pail down and smiled.

"What's the moral of the story?" the professor asked. The students thought about this for a moment before answering.

"If you try harder, you can do more!" said one student.

"There is always a way to fit more into your schedule!" said another.

"We have all the time we need to get things done!" cried a third.

The professor nodded. "These are all good points," he commented, "but they are not the true moral of the story. The moral of the story is: ***if you don't put the big rocks in the jar FIRST, you won't get them all back in."***

The wisdom of this story is revealed when you consider the examples in reverse. If you put the water in first, then the sand, then the gravel and then try to replace the big rocks, you will find that the big rocks won't all fit. Remember, these rocks were originally in the jar and did fit if you put them in first. This is a

> ***If you don't put the BIG rocks in the jar FIRST, you get them all back in.***
> **-Stephen Covey**

perfect analogy to how most people structure their day: they do everything unimportant and trivial *first* (the sand, water and gravel) and try to attempt their biggest priorities *last* (the big rocks). In fact, most of the time, people never even have room in their schedule for the big rocks at all. The biggest priorities in their lives, including their marriage, relationships with kids, health and fitness, creative projects, personal and career development, are all the big rocks that get left out on a daily basis. **The key to getting things done is to put the big rocks in the jar *first*.**

How do You Evaluate and Determine Priorities?

"It is the mark of great people to treat trifles as trifles and important matters as important."
- Doris Lessing

One of the challenges with accomplishing your "big rocks" is that you first need to decide how to determine whether something is a priority or not. Are you reacting to the emergency of the moment, or does this goal fit into your long-term plan? In order to do this, we need a system for evaluating and categorizing priorities.

Alan Lakein, an authority on time management, popularized the "To-Do list" and the concept of categorizing things according to priority: things that must be done today would be labeled "A", things that would be nice to have accomplished today would be labeled "B" and the remaining miscellaneous tasks would be labeled "C". This certainly revolutionized the concept of organizing around priorities, but this strategy has one major flaw: you focus primarily on today's emergencies, the "A" tasks, while potentially ignoring the opportunities of tomorrow, the "B" tasks. The challenge with this is that if you leave a "B" task undone for a long enough period, it eventually becomes today's emergency... and you are running around every day putting out fires instead of getting quality work done ahead of schedule. This system of "A-B-C" categorization is good but can be dramatically improved upon.

Stephen Covey improved upon these criteria with his model of "Importance vs. Urgency" is his popular book "The Seven Habits of Highly Effective People", using the two criteria (Time and Value) to delineate four distinct quadrants. These quadrants are **Time-Sensitive and High-Value** (today's emergencies), **Not Time-Sensitive but High-Value** (future opportunities, long-term projects and personal growth), **Time-Sensitive and Low Value** (distractions, interruptions and other peoples emergencies) and tasks that are **NOT Time-Sensitive and Low Value** (wasted time).

In order to apply this method of categorizing your own priorities, you need to examine the tasks on your "to do" list. The first question you need to ask yourself is: which are the criteria you will use to evaluate your priorities? This is a critical first step, for most people fail to utilize effective criteria. Usually the first and most common criterion is simply the deadline: when is this task due? This is a very easy criteria to measure, since you have a quantifiable criteria built in: a time and date. Something that is due in 5 minutes will likely harness your attention and energies over something due 5 months from now.

You might refer to your second criteria as "importance" or "value". This criterion is wide open to interpretation and therefore equally open to excellent definitions as it is weak ones. Some people determine that the tasks they should accomplish first are the ones that are the most fun to do. Others might believe that the ones that are the easiest or can be accomplished fastest should be tackled first. Many times our emotions cloud our judgment; we might have co-workers who are difficult to get along with, and we choose to do tasks in order of who will yell the loudest if they aren't accomplished. We know that Brian will kick up a real fuss if his report isn't finished quickly, whereas Ted will roll over and shrug. Brian's report gets the focus, whether it has the higher value or not.

A more effective definition of 'valuable' might be to focus on what the return on investment is. If one task yields $1000 of revenue and takes 5 minutes, and a second task yields the same income but takes a month, the obvious answer is to do the 5 minute task, and then find thousands more examples just like it to do over and over.

Maybe value lies in the relationship that you will build: you accomplish a task that generates no immediate revenue, but solidifies a working relationship with a potentially huge new client that will triple your business this year.

Every task that we do can be measured in how time-sensitive and valuable it is, and it will fall somewhere on the chart below. I don't believe that you can categorize something simply as "important" or "not-important" as Covey does in his model (and I realize he only does this for simplicity in his explanation). I believe that it is more pragmatic to think of things along a scale of 1-10. So, on a scale of 1-10, how time-sensitive and how valuable is the task?

Section 1: Time-Sensitive and High-Value. These are all of the tasks that MUST be done, right now. They are mission-critical, life-and-death, schedule-ruining emergencies. These are all of the things that when they happen, whatever else you had planned to do gets cancelled. Things that would fall into this category would be a car accident, a rush to the emergency room, a sudden recall on food products from grocery store shelves, or your top client is about to quit your firm if you don't finish this last-minute report by 5pm. These things must be dealt with immediately. We've all had days where you have a schedule carefully laid out, and by 10am your schedule has been ruined by an unexpected problem that must be addressed.

After any emergency, it's always valuable to do a post-mortem and ask "why did this happen?" If the emergency has occurred before, and you can reasonably predict it will happen again, try to identify any assignable cause. Is it something that you personally caused, through procrastination, disorganization, or poor communication? If you had no hand in causing the emergency, then who did? Try to identify the source of the emergency, and if another person was the cause, try to connect with them to understand why it happened and how it could be averted in the future.

Section 2: NOT Time-Sensitive and High-Value. These are all of the tasks that MUST be done, but you don't have to do them today. In fact, it might be days, weeks, months or even years before you have to do them. This would include saving for retirement, exercising regularly, recharging your batteries with high-quality leisure activities, spending quality time with your family and nurturing those relationships, personal and professional development like attending night school or seminars on the weekend, reading books to improve your skills and wisdom, planning for the future, role-playing and developing plans to prevent and respond to potential emergencies, and more. This is the section with the greatest opportunity for massive positive results, but it also invites the greatest problems. Because you don't have to do these tasks today, the tendency for most people is to procrastinate. But when you procrastinate on taking care of your health, or your retirement savings, or your marriage, you can cause irreparable damage. If you leave one of these tasks long enough without addressing it, eventually you wake up and it has become today's emergency!

Section 3: Time-Sensitive and Low-Value. These are all of the interruptions, distractions, and other people's emergencies. You would see this happening when you are having dinner with your family, and the telephone rings with someone offering to sell you a newspaper subscription. The phone might be ringing urgently, but it really doesn't matter and it probably isn't more important than dinner with your family. But many people tend to respond to things that happen right now, because people confuse urgency with importance. Another example would be people interrupting you at work to solve their problems. Most of the time this is perfectly acceptable, but let's suppose you are under a tight deadline and are involved in very creative work. It takes a certain amount of time to get into "flow" state where ideas come quickly and naturally, and if you get interrupted you literally have to start over, re-acclimate your mind to what you were working on, review all of your notes… and time is lost.

A final example of Section 3 tasks would be caused by someone's inability to say the word "no". Many people, particularly those with a passive personality, fear saying the word no because they believe that if they don't say yes then the other person will be mad at them. So they say yes to chairing the Parent-Teacher Association, running the United Way fundraising drive, baking cookies for the soccer team, organizing the pot luck brunch for the Holidays, staying late to finish other people's work, etc. At a certain point, you MUST say no to other people's requests, because it is physically impossible to say yes to everything. You will stretch yourself to the point of mediocrity if you try to be everything for everybody.

Section 4: NOT Time-Sensitive and Low-Value. This is wasted time. This would include sitting around, mindlessly flipping channels in front of the TV for hours, etc. Nothing of value is accomplished in this category. However, here is an interesting question to ponder: is it possible to be working hard at something, and actually WASTE time? Absolutely! How might you do that? There are dozens of reasons, but here are a few examples:

1. Spending time trying to figure out something through trial-and error, when you could simply pick up the phone and ask.
2. Unknowingly working on a less-important task because you have not prioritized your tasks carefully enough
3. Having a disorganized work station where you spend time looking for important documents
4. Inefficient processes, like sifting through mountains of paper document files when all of these files can be digitized for instantaneous file retrieval
5. Picking up a piece of paper, looking at it, resolving to do it later, then putting it down
6. A coworker at your office has a 3-day service-level agreement to complete a task. After 1 day, they finish the task, but will not submit the work before the end of the 3 days because they don't want you to start expecting them to work any faster the next time they have to complete the same task.
7. Being TIRED. If you are exhausted, your productivity plummets, and it takes you longer to accomplish a task. That's why it is so foolish to skip your lunch break. You aren't being more productive, you're being less productive because you've chosen to not rest and refill. If you're tired, it takes you 8 hours to do six hours of work. If you're energized, it takes you 5 hours to do 6 hours of work. Add an extra hour

for lunch, and you're still two hours ahead. Corporate North America needs to get over the ridiculous optics of sitting at your desk working through lunch so that the department can see how committed you are to your job. Take a break and get more work done; stop wasting time by choosing to be hungry and tired.

8. Productive Procrastination: You need to do something, you schedule time to work on it, you have all of the information and tools you need, there is no one interrupting you… but you just don't want to work on the task! So what do you do? ANYTHING ELSE! You tidy your desk, your garage, you do any menial less-important task to distract yourself and trick everyone into believing you are doing what you are supposed to be doing!

These are all excellent examples of wasting time!

Time Management Self-Quiz

"Time is a great teacher, but unfortunately it kills all its pupils."
- Hector Louis Berlioz

So, the question is: how good are you at prioritization? Do you do the most important "big-rocks" first, or do you tackle the gravel, sand and water tasks? Take a moment and consider the following examples. Check off every example that seems to describe you, and then add up your answers below. This can give you some insight into how you manage your priorities!

Section "A" situations:

- ❑ I work best when I'm under pressure
- ❑ Whenever there is an emergency, I'm usually the most qualified person to jump in and "save the day"
- ❑ I can't be thinking about what problems might be coming down the pike… I've got to focus solely on solving *today's* problems!
- ❑ If something is happening "Right now", that automatically means that it is important!
- ❑ I often skip lunch and get the work done… lunch can wait.
- ❑ I feel that good customer service means that every time a client say's "Jump", I ask "How high?!"
- ❑ Making a schedule for the day is useless, because there's always another crisis to deal with.
- ❑ I love the adrenaline rush I get from putting out "fires".
- ❑ If I didn't solve a huge emergency today, my day feels empty.
- ❑ People are less important than deadlines.

Section "B" situations:

- ❑ I build my schedule around my most important tasks

- ❑ Because of careful planning and organization, I routinely finish work before it is due
- ❑ I like to schedule time to plan ahead
- ❑ I look to see if there are any potential problems that might soon grow into an emergency, and I work to prevent them.
- ❑ I am aware of spontaneous opportunities to network, and like to build better working relationships with colleagues.
- ❑ I build in a "buffer zone" in all of my planning, so in case I am running behind on a project, I am still able to meet deadlines.
- ❑ After an emergency, I spend a few moments considering either possible back-up plans to stop that type of emergency from occurring again, or ways of reducing the impact of a similar future emergency.
- ❑ I routinely take a lunch break and enjoy some balance in the middle of my day.
- ❑ I am effective at minimizing or eliminating "wasted time"
- ❑ If my job description allows it, I routinely schedule time in my office that I am not to be interrupted, to focus on upcoming projects and reports.
- ❑ I analyze opportunities and create strategies for success
- ❑ I champion continuous improvement in my personal and professional life

Section "C" situations:

- ❑ If someone asks me to help them with their work, I feel guilty if I say "No"

- ❑ I can't really plan my day around "priorities"... because *everything* is a priority!
- ❑ I'm frequently involved in meetings that have no clear agenda, and trail off into tangents that don't seem relevant to me.
- ❑ Whenever a co-worker needs assistance, I am there to help out, even if it isn't my direct responsibility
- ❑ Whenever I see that I have email waiting, I love to open it immediately and see who needs me. What if it's really important to them? I wouldn't want to keep them waiting.
- ❑ I routinely volunteer for responsibilities that are not part of my job description.
- ❑ If somebody stops by my desk to ask a question, but they want to tell me all about their weekend, it feels rude to just get down to business.
- ❑ I am often unsure as to what priorities I should focus on.
- ❑ I have a hard time cutting people off if they are long-winded, and making me late for an important meeting.
- ❑ I answer the phone immediately when it rings; you never know who could need me!

Section "D" situations:

- ❑ I tend to procrastinate on tasks at work.
- ❑ When starting a phone call, I usually like to "visit" with the person on the phone and socialize, before getting down to business.
- ❑ I frequently find myself unable to focus on the task at hand.

- ❑ I'd rather keep busy working on something I know is less important, so at least it *looks* like I'm working hard.
- ❑ Whenever a friend sends me an email, I like to read it right away.
- ❑ Chatting at the water cooler or coffee machine is a great way to meet new friends, and a nice way to relax during the day.
- ❑ I tend to be slow to starting on projects or work I don't like, even though I know I should get busy on them.
- ❑ I tend to waste time on *worrying* about getting a task done, rather than just simply taking action.
- ❑ I often have a sense that I should be working on a bigger, more important task, but I don't feel like it at that moment. I'd rather do something quick and easy.
- ❑ I like to surf the internet for fun at work.

Check all the examples that apply. How did you score? Add up your check marks and fill in the results to determine in which section you spend the majority of your time!

Section A: _____ Section B: _____
Section C: _____Section D: _____

TOP TIME-WASTING EXCUSES

"If you haven't got the time to do it right, when will you find the time to do it over?"
- Jeffery J. Mayer

"An alarm clock is a device that makes you rise and whine."
- Author Unknown

The primary challenge with managing time is NOT that it is a finite resource, but that you own responsibility for using it well. Recognize that all behavior (productive or not) and decisions (conscientious or not) ultimately stem from you thoughts. Effective thinking yields effective results. Rather than deride the universe for not bequeathing you with an extra hour to get it all done, take responsibility and search inside for the ingrained beliefs that are holding you back from making the most of your day.

> *The primary challenge with managing time is NOT that it is a finite resource, but that you own responsibility for using it well.*
> **-CJ Calvert**

Time management is a game that you will play against yourself; against your own mind. It's a complete head game. And what you are competing against is not your calendar, but your own thinking. Your decisions, your strengths and weaknesses, your impulses, your motivation, your value system, your ability to say NO to wasteful things and

YES to purposeful things are what will transform your effectiveness. It is a game that is played, that is won and lost, on a battleground that is six inches wide, between your own ears.

With even a cursory examination, we can identify some of the most common errors in thinking that lead to time being wasted. Consider the following examples; you may come to find that some of these debilitating beliefs may have creeped into your thinking.

- ***Excuse #1: I don't have enough time.*** Franklin Field says: *"The great dividing line between success and failure can be expressed in five words: I DID NOT HAVE TIME."* How many dreams have been buried, never to see the light of day, because the dreamer was consumed with minutia and diversion? J.K. Rowling, billionaire author of the Harry Potter series of books, is the top-selling author of all time. People might assume that in order to write the best-selling books, she had all the spare time in the world. The opposite is true. Unemployed at the time, she would wait for her baby girl to fall asleep before going down to a coffee shop and writing feverishly into the night. She could have used her situation as an excuse, she could have said she was too tired to write, too broke, too demoralized, but she did not. She *made* the time, and the rest is history.

  We may not have all of the time we want to do everything we want. But we can always find *some* time to do the things most important to us. You have some spare moments that are underutilized, and you can make better use of them. There are some individuals who are in truly challenging situations. Perhaps you are a single mother working 3 jobs to pay for food and rent. Perhaps your spouse is lying on a hospital bed after major surgery and you leave work every day and spend all evening by their bedside, praying for their recovery. These are very extreme situations, and are clearly more challenging to manage through. But unless you are in the midst of an all consuming emergency, the hum-drum pattern of many days leaves incredible opportunity for achievement if we were only to step up.

Excuse #2: I promise I'll start later. Really? At what time, and what is the written consequence that you are publicly accountable to if you don't deliver? This is the GREATEST time management psychological fallacy. A. B. Zu Tavern says *"If, before going to bed every night, you will tear a page from the calendar, and remark, "there goes another day of my life, never to return," you will become time conscious."* Mass billions of people delude themselves into believing that they will take action 'tomorrow'. The problem is, tomorrow never comes, for when we wake up tomorrow, we will re-name it "today". Everything you ever do to improve your lot in life will happen during a "today". If you are to

> *"Today's greatest labor-saving device is tomorrow."*
> **- Woodrow Wilson**

harness your talents, channel your energies, transform your body and marriage and finances, you will do all of these things during a "today". By using this ridiculous excuse, you delude yourself into thinking that you haven't really slacked off because you've made a mental resolution to take action. In fact, the very act of making the decision to act tomorrow almost FEELS like you've really been proactive. In the words of Woodrow Wilson *"Today's greatest labor-saving device is tomorrow."* But you're kidding yourself, and your conscience is probably rolling its eyes when you use this flimsy resolution.

- ***Excuse #3: I work better under pressure.*** Some people believe that leaving things to the last minute and then racing full-steam to reach a deadline will assure them of exceptional performance. Perhaps you've had experiences where the heat was on, you had to pull a rabbit out of the hat, and you were victorious. What happens in this situation? Well, on the positive side you form a positive "Victory" reference that will give you energy and courage in tough moments and allow you to face future emergencies with a greater sense of calm and efficacy. However, this is a double-edged sword, for you may begin to believe that you can ONLY work in high-pressure situations. Perhaps the underlying truth is that you need external deadlines to motivate yourself. Maybe you've pulled it off enough times that you start cutting yourself some scheduling slack, thinking *"Hey, I don't need to start working on this project now… I can leave it till the night before and pound off a decent report… After all, I've done it before."* Consider this: can you intellectually agree that if you had time to double-check your work, you might be able to improve the quality? The answer is a resounding yes.

- ***Excuse #4: I can do it better/faster myself.*** Leadership demands that you set the example for your team. Management demands that you guide your staff to delivering what is expected of them. What usually happens for people in positions of leadership is that they have graduated up through the ranks because of the expertise and effectiveness they've shown at their job, the job that is currently being done by their staff or team. Of course, you can do their job better or faster than they can: that's why you're the manager. However, you have a finite number of hours in the day. Once you exceed physical capacity, you collapse. The only way to accomplish more is to train-up a farm team of new superstars in order to duplicate yourself and your time. And, to do that, you have to grit your teeth and suffer through the growing pains of their learning and development. If you keep jumping in and doing the work for them, you are forever chained to mediocrity and will never advance.

- ***Excuse #5: I don't want to let other people down.*** It can be emotionally difficult to say

"No" to other people's requests, particularly when you care for them and they have helped you out in times of need. The question always remains: what is the #1 thing you should be working on right now? Does that person's emergency supercede your greatest pre-determined priority? Will your relationship suffer if you do not help them, and is that the higher priority than the task on which you are focused? These are the variables that you must consider. The most common reaction for people is to put everyone else FIRST, and to put their individual priorities dead LAST. And frankly, that is a fantastic way to never accomplish anything of lasting value. Consider even the nobility of the person who dedicates their life to the charitable work of serving others. If you NEVER stop to eat and sleep, if you NEVER stop and say "no" to others at least once in a while, you will burn out and lose all efficacy. John Wanamaker *says "People who cannot find time for recreation are obliged sooner or later to find time for illness."* Sometimes, the only way to honor the people you love is to say "no" to them today so that you may recharge your own vital batteries and rise to serve them again tomorrow.

> ***"People who cannot find time for recreation are obliged sooner or later to find time for illness."***
> **- John Wanamaker**

- ***Excuse #6: I don't* want *to do this.*** Realistically, you wouldn't allow your 2-year-old child to use this excuse if it meant neglecting anything of importance. Why would you accept this from yourself when shirking your responsibilities? Not wanting to do something is a useful criterion only if the question is *"What would I like to do for fun?"* Aside from that, it is almost never a valid criterion when discussing your identified priorities. The only question that champions ask in this situation is "What result do I want?" They never ask "What program would require the least effort?" and choose their goals based on that. But too many people subjugate their deepest priorities for the distractions and pleasures of the moment. People of integrity do what they know must be done. They don't sip from the shallow mud-puddle of immediate gratification, but rather drink from the well of duty to inform them of their course. They celebrate virtues such as honor, responsibility, achievement and long-term vision and use these values as a catalyst for action when their temptations for weakness and leisure are too distracting.

- ***Excuse #7: I'm too TIRED right now.*** Unfortunately, it's not uncommon for people to feel exhausted in our modern society (not that any time in history has been different!) People don't fuel their body with proper nutritious food, they have poor sleeping habits, they don't exercise regularly, and the task they must accomplish may be emotionally and psychologically exhausting if it doesn't match their skill set. However, sometimes you've got to push through fatigue and do it anyway. This doesn't contradict my earlier point about the value of taking a break to recharge; what I mean here is that once you've taken a break, you can't just keep taking breaks all day until you feel rested. That's called a vacation, and you're not likely going to get a week-long Hawaiian vacation every time you're sleepy! If you still feel tired after your break, a MAJOR Section B task is to quickly identify what's missing from your diet, fitness or sleep habits and correct it immediately. While you're looking for those important answers, however, you simply have to shoulder some responsibility in your life and complete the task you were assigned. It won't get easier if you leave it for later, it just gets harder. Sometimes, champions fight on even when they're running on empty.

All of these might seem like valid explanations at the moment, but many times they are just excuses for why you won't perform and succeed. Once you have cleared your mental garden of all the weeds of negative thinking towards managing time, you can get serious about understanding how to take action.

PLANNING YOUR SCHEDULE

Time Blocks

"In truth, people can generally make time for what they choose to do; it is not really the time but the will that is lacking."
- Sir John Lubbock

Stephen Covey popularized this concept in his wonderful book, "First Things First". The concept is quite simple: imagine that you have a regular appointment, let's say a date night each weekend with your spouse. You've decided that this is clearly a priority and you want to make time for your relationship. What you do is schedule a date for yourselves, and you keep that date fixed in your calendar so that when other lesser priorities threaten to cancel your date, you say "no" to the lesser priority.

The challenge with life is that we have to allow some flexibility and adjust to the reality of a busy life filled with multiple priorities. I'll give you an example. As I'm writing this, my wife and I are heading out to have dinner and catch a movie; we're dropping our little boy off with my parents so that we have a night to ourselves. As much as I love my wife (and I do) the way my brain works is that I need to write things into my calendar. I don't know about you, but if I verbally commit to something but don't put it into the calendar, sometimes I forget and I end up disappointing people. So, everything goes into the calendar.

If I don't put the phrase "DATE NIGHT" into my calendar, what foreseeable problem may arise? Well, one of my friends might call me up and say "Hey CJ, lets get together and have fun." No problem. But I place top priority on having some time with my sweetheart, so I want to make sure that each week that gets taken care of first before I hang out with my friends. So, if a friend calls up and says "Let's get together Saturday and play some pool or watch a movie" I just look in my calendar and say "Oh, sorry buddy, it's date night for us... How about Friday?" This way my highest priority, my wife, is taken care of.

Now, suppose something happens that supercedes the date? My grandparents celebrated their 60th wedding anniversary last January. We had family from all over North America fly in to celebrate! They received written congratulations from the Queen of England, the Prime Minister, the Premier, and on down the line. However, when they called, I did NOT say "Oh, I'd love to come and celebrate with you, but my wife and I are going to be catching a movie that night!" Clearly, a once-in-a-lifetime celebration like this takes the priority.

So, here is where the concept of a "Time Block" comes in. You don't ever cancel a scheduled priority if something bigger comes up; you simply shift the Time Block to another time. So, we went to my Grandparents celebration on Saturday, shifted our date to Friday night, and I cancelled whatever plans I had scheduled with my buddies on Friday night. My bride is a greater priority than my friends! You always want to honor your priorities in their order of importance, to ensure the most important things get done.

This is an example of my own regular time blocks through the week. To be realistic, this isn't always how my week plays out, but that's the point of time blocks. If something else happens, I still try to honor all of my priorities but I may shift the time that I had planned to do so. Writing doesn't have an assigned time because it gets planned around my speaking schedule, which is different every single day. Writing is a Section B activity and speaking is Section A, but my speaking engagements have concrete times assigned to them whereas writing is flexible in its timing. Also, my passionate hobby is composing symphony music (which is what I majored in during my time in University). I like to play the piano daily, but sitting down to really dig into my hobby and write is something saved for the weekend when I've got some quiet time (which is very interesting to manage with a 1-year old baby!)

PRIORITY:	Mon	Tues	Wed	Thurs	Fri	Sat	Sun
Date Night					6-10pm	Alt.	
Spouse	night	night	night	night		night	night
Time with baby	7am	7am	7am	7am	7am	7am	7am
Business Association				7-10pm			
Exercise			5:30pm			8:30am	
Extended Family							5-9pm
Admin						Alt.	9
Spouse Time off							12-5 pm
Writing	?	?	?	?	?	?	?
Housework							9-11 am
Music composition						?	?

Focus on Your #1 Task

"The first hour of the morning is the rudder of the day."
- Henry Ward Beecher

Writing any book is an exercise in overcoming procrastination, at building your schedule around your top priority, and keeping yourself energized and thinking clearly to produce quality work. I endeavor to practice what I preach, and you wouldn't be reading this book if I didn't follow my own time-management advice. To say that I attacked this book and hammered it out quickly might be an understatement: only *two chapters* were written prior to 3 weeks before the date I have submitted this book to the publisher; **aside from two chapters, every word of this book was written in *18 days*,** from

October 16th to November 2nd, 2008, and even those two finished chapters needed polishing, editing and further writing. During these 18 days, I also went to my 5 regular gym workouts, celebrated my Mother's birthday, celebrated my anniversary with my wife by taking her to the theatre production of "Dirty Dancing" in Toronto, enjoyed a dinner-and-movie date with my wife, celebrated my son's 1st birthday with 30 friends and family in our home, spent at least an hour every day in quality time with my son and wife, took my baby son out Trick-or-Treating for Halloween, went to 2 industry association meetings, and delivered 17 presentations to corporate clients.

My point in sharing this example is that I hear people tell me that they *have no time to accomplish things*. You know what I didn't do in the last 17 days? Laundry. Or mow the lawn. I also ignored the dishes in our sink. You know why I didn't do those things? Because to me, they were the *dead last priorities* on my list. I hired a cleaning lady so my sweetheart wasn't carrying the load by herself. So many people dream of writing a book, or climbing a mountain, or building a school in a third-world country, or building a business, but they just can't seem to find the time with their "busy schedule". They are busy with water, gravel and sand. **Successful people don't get a lot of trivial things done, because they're too busy accomplishing MAJOR GOALS**. The only way that I wrote 80% of a book in 18 days, while continuing to maintain the major priorities in my life, is that I **determine the #1 task for each day and do it first**.

> ***"Successful people don't get a lot of trivial things done, because they're too busy accomplishing MAJOR GOALS."***
> - CJ Calvert

Consider the following scenario: Have you ever had a day at work where you raced from one meeting to the next, sent a blizzard of emails, didn't even stop for lunch, spent your entire day fighting one emergency after the other, and you arrive home at night utterly exhausted emotionally and physically… and yet you feel like you accomplished… *nothing*. Has this ever happened to you? There is a simple reason, and a simple remedy.

The reason that you feel like you have accomplished nothing is because you have focused on your less important tasks at the expense of your most important tasks. The solution, quite simply, is to reverse this formula: do the most important thing first. This is such a simple and foundational principle of effective time management, and yet it is violated on a daily basis by almost every human being alive. **Do the most important thing first**, and you will never again suffer a day of your life that you feel has been wasted.

Decide in your own mind, preferably before you go to bed the night before, what the #1 greatest priority is of tomorrow. **If you only accomplish one single thing, what MUST you accomplish tomorrow?** If nothing else is finished, what is of critical unyielding importance? That is your #1 priority.

Now, the game begins. Suppose that we are referring to a day at the office. Your first challenge is this: When you walk into the office, **how many minutes does it take for you to START working on your #1 priority?** Is it 5 minutes? 27 minutes? 3 hours? Most people, if they are proactive enough to even have a priority that they are focused on, will usually start working on that task by the mid-afternoon. After every distracting email, impromptu conversation, unscheduled 20 minute meeting and coffee break, 2pm rolls around and you have yet to begin on your #1 task. So my challenge to you is this: begin immediately. Don't check your voice mail or email. Don't get a coffee and glance at the morning paper. Go directly to your desk, and begin working on your #1 priority.

Here is the second challenge: **How many minutes can you stay focused on your #1 priority before you get distracted?** 5 minutes? 14 minutes? 46 minutes? This is where the word "no" becomes powerful and liberating, because most everything else that might be a possible interruption is less important than what you are working on right now.

The key to keeping your focus on your #1 priority is to **set up a meeting with yourself**. Imagine what would happen to your productivity if you had no interruptions and no distractions; if you were literally left alone to focus on the task at hand. Would your productivity increase? Most likely, your productivity would soar. So, schedule a meeting with yourself and treat it as if you were meeting with the president of your organization. What interruptions would be acceptable if you were meeting with your president? Perhaps a call from you child's school saying they had been injured, or something else of that magnitude. All other 'emergencies' can wait 30 minutes. Remember, just because something is an emergency to someone else does not necessarily determine that it is an emergency to *you*. You have already determined your #1 priority for the day.

If the telephone rings when you are in a meeting, is it acceptable that it goes to voicemail? In most cases, yes (unless you are a 9-1-1 telephone operator or receptionist). If you are on the phone with another client and the phone rings, the call goes to voicemail and this is also acceptable. You do not need to interrupt your focus just because the phone has rung; record your outgoing message to indicate that you will pick up messages in 30 minutes and be free of concern. Besides, if something is a legitimate emergency, no one will be satisfied with simply leaving a voicemail; they will continue to call back every minute until they get you or a colleague on the phone, and they will instruct someone to walk over to your desk and interrupt you.

Make Use Of Spare Moments

"Guard well your spare moments. They are like uncut diamonds. Discard them and their value will never be known. Improve them and they will become the brightest gems in a useful life."
- Ralph Waldo Emerson

Once you've filled in the big rocks into your calendar, it's time to get down to the gravel, sand and water. All of the little things you need to accomplish have to eventually find their way onto your calendar, but always remember that they don't go on the list until the big rocks are all accounted for. The only time I scheduled time for a low-priority task is if I've neglected it for so long that it has started to shift in importance and urgency, and it's becoming a

> ***"It has been my observation that most people get ahead during the time that others waste."***
> **- Henry Ford**

problem. Then I plan some time, batch all of the work together, do it all in one blast and I'm done with it.

People who really get ahead seem to be masters at making the most of everything they've got, including spare moments. Let's suppose you have 10 minutes before you must start your next scheduled task. It's 1:50pm. What do you do? Most people waste the time and blow their opportunity to get ahead. They get a coffee, chit-chat, surf the net, scan the newspaper, etc. What could you do? If you had 10 spare minutes (which all of us have in multiples, even if we don't recognize it) what would you do with it? I'd recommend that you have a couple of key things ready to go at any time when you've got 10 minutes, such as filing, ordering your office supplies, reading your "fyi" emails, etc. Call it your "Sand & Water" list. That way, when you find you've got some extra time, you aren't fussing around wondering what to do; you just look at your list and knock off a couple of quick tasks. Henry Ford says *"It has been my observation that most people get ahead during the time that others waste."*

Superstars Build Networks In Advance

Time management has a lot to do with how effective you are in your interaction with people: if you have prioritized and blocked aside time to have a meeting with a colleague to discuss an urgent matter, the time will be effective if you have proactively made deposits in the relationship before hand. If you are going into the meeting and the climate is one of dislike or, even worse, a climate of distrust, you can prioritize and schedule meetings and block time very methodically all you want. The time won't be effective.

Daniel Goleman, author of Emotional Intelligence says: "during normal activities, the normal networks are effective. But during times of crisis, the informal networks kick in, and are suprisingly effective. People are organized into three networks: communication (who talks to whom) [COMRADERIE], Expertise networks, i.e. who knows the technical answers and provides them, [COMPETENCE] and Trust networks [CONFIDENCE]. "Star performers... do the work of building reliable networks before they actually need them. When they call someone for advice, stars almost always get a faster answer."

High-Leverage spontaneous interaction with people, to get to know them and build a relationship, is a huge deposit in their emotional bank account. Making these deposits spontaneously allows you to be more effective with them, particularly when you must make an urgent request of them.

OVERCOMING PROCRASTINATION

"There are those of us who are always about to live. We are waiting until things change, until there is more time, until we are less tired, until we get a promotion, until we settle down -- until, until, until. It always seems as if there is some major event that must occur in our lives before we begin living."
- George Sheehan

What Is Procrastination?

"Procrastination causes all of life's emergencies."
- Dr. Steve Stokl

Once you have settled your mind on a task and resolved to see it to completion… once you have organized your calendar around that priority and protected time to accomplish it…once you are sitting at your desk, or staring at your messy garage, or contemplating the file-folder of bills that need to be organized to file your taxes, one final ingredient remains: you must now take action.

What causes people to procrastinate? Understand that procrastination is an emotional experience. At some level, you believe that doing something right now will be very uncomfortable, and doing it later would be more pleasant. Or you are comparing two tasks to determine which one you would enjoy more: watching television or taking out the garbage; eating a salad versus eating a chocolate bar; facing the challenge in your marriage and having an important conversation, or avoiding all connection. Napoleon

Bonaparte says ***"There are two levers for moving men -- interest and fear."*** Tony Robbins refers to these levers as "pain" and "pleasure". Everything that we do stems from the desire to get pleasure or avoid pain.

STEP 1: Increase the PLEASURE you get from the activity. Give yourself a powerful and motivating reason to take action now. You've probably already done this in some fashion before; you may have resolved to push on for another 20 minutes of focused effort and then reward yourself with a coffee break. Ask yourself "How can I make this activity more fun/ enjoyable/ rewarding?" Brainstorm small rewards that you can use to treat yourself when you perform. It might be a favorite activity, or a food, or a television show. Maybe you treat yourself to a small gift as a reward when you accomplish the task at hand. Whatever the reward, if it is more compelling than the discomfort of the work itself, you will take action. If the reward does not serve to stir your passions, then consider increasing it. If this still does not work, then you must follow...

> *"There are two levers for moving men -- interest and fear."*
> **- Napoleon Bonaparte**

STEP 2: Increase the CONSEQUENCE if you don't take action. Remarkably, many people are far more motivated by a deadline with a consequence than with rewards. For example, many people struggle with exercise and say *"I don't have time"*. This is the most common excuse given, yet it is rarely true. In reality, the actual excuse is usually *"I don't feel like exercising; it's uncomfortable, and besides I'd rather watch TV and eat potato chips on the couch."* It feels more pleasurable to bask in leisure, so they do so. However, consider the mindset of a middle-aged man who has just suffered a heart attack. He sits down with his doctor and is told that he must immediately stop smoking, cut out all the fatty red meat and begin jogging 30 minutes every day. If he doesn't do this, he is told that he will likely endure another heart attack and risk his life.

Well, the same man who said "I don't have time to jog" on Monday can be seen out running on the track on Tuesday. What changed? Did his schedule all of a sudden open up and all his appointments cleared? No. All it took was a heart attack to motivate him, and miraculously he finds the time to jog. He always had the time; it just wasn't important enough to do. People seem to leap into action whenever a deadline is looming. Many people file their taxes the week they are due. Many students write their term papers the week they are due (or the evening before!). It seems that the painful consequence attached to a looming deadline is a remarkable inspiration to many.

Tips on Overcoming Procrastination

"Are you in earnest? Seize this very minute! Boldness has genius, power, and magic in it. Only engage, and then the mind grows heated. Begin, and then the work will be completed."
- John Anster

- **Manage 'overwhelm' by taking small bites.** Sometimes the task at hand seems so big that we don't know where to begin. We spend time simply looking at the pile of boxes and ruminating to ourselves "What a mess!" and feel we can't start until we decide exactly which box is the correct box to unpack and sort through. Pick one and stick with it until you've finished; don't be pulled off track and drift into sorting through others. If you worry that you might miss something, take out a piece of paper and write down everything that you need to do. Don't leave out a single detail. Next, prioritize the list and decide the first thing you must do on the list. Then, fold up the paper, put it in your pocket and just do the first thing on the list. That's it. Once you've completed your task, unfold the paper and cross off that action item. Now, you're beginning to see some progress. You will feel a sense of mastery and control over your life as you methodically check off one item after another, and soon the mountainous pile of tasks has been eroded.

- **Create your accountability team.** As with any goal, one of the most powerful motivators is to tell other people that you have a goal to accomplish and that you will accomplish it. Make a commitment to someone whose love and respect for you is so important that the thought of disappointing them would crush you. Promise them that you will follow through on your task. Then, report back to the people you've promised to tell them that you accomplished the task… or did not. Silence suggests failure, and they'll know you didn't follow through. Admit your procrastination to others publicly. Don't cop out on this: if you didn't finish, you have to face the music. The discomfort of doing this (hopefully) should propel you not to miss the deadline again.

- **Schedule 10 minutes to begin your task.** If 'busyness' is the excuse, schedule just 10 minutes to get going. You can't rationalize that you don't have 10 minutes, and you'll find that once you get the ball rolling it's pretty easy to get the job done. As well, with a short deadline you might be inspired to give 110% for those 10 minutes and really get some work done.

- **Focus your mind on the positives of finishing the task (and the negatives of staying the same).** Rather than thinking about how unpleasant it is to do something, focus your mind on how good you will feel when you finish! How proud you will be of yourself, how you will hold up in the eyes of your friends and loved ones. Review movies in your mind of other times you have finished things and then felt a sense of pride and peace; now you have earned the time to rest. Taking a break when we really deserve it is always 100 times more rewarding than indulging in the same leisure activity when we know we have work to do. When we make this mistake, our pleasure is clouded by guilt and anxiety, and we never quite get to relax and enjoy ourselves. Keep your mind focused on the prize at the end of the race and you'll stay motivated.

- **Resolve that a person of your character is above this behavior.** You're too good to fall into the trap of mediocrity. You know that you are capable of more, and you are letting yourself down if you don't take action, not to mention letting your loved ones down. People are counting on you and looking up to you because of the example you have set. Honour their belief in you and always be the best, most productive person you can be.

- **Change your language to that of a winner**. Champions say "I'll make it happen." They say "I'll find the time," "This is important", and "Work before play". Those who struggle with accomplishing their goals do not.

- **Take action now.** Don't hesitate for a moment. As my wife jokes "If you have to procrastinate, just procrastinate later."

- **Don't allow perfectionism to paralyze you; temporarily lower your standards in order to get the ball rolling.** If you are consumed with doing things 'perfectly', you are in for a rude awakening. Perfection is the endlessly retreating horizon; you can run your entire life and exhaust yourself and you will never ever reach it. If you have identified this as your problem, commit to doing a 'rough draft' where you are not accountable to your standards of perfectionism. Sometimes, you need to do a 'decent' job in order to begin moving in the direction of an 'excellent' one.

- **Create a journal to identify exactly what is holding you back.** Strategies are ineffective unless they are used appropriately. You must accurately diagnose the problem in order to prescribe the appropriate course of action to remedy it. Ask yourself "Why am I leaving this for later? Why can't I do this right now? What will happen if I do it right now? How will I feel?" Introspection like this is simultaneously demanding and highly beneficial. Imagine if the reason you were procrastinating was fear, and you weren't doing anything to address the fear that you felt. Every other well-intentioned time management tip would be wasted, and you'd end up wasting a lot of your time trying them.

> *Most of the current quality of your life has come from past moments of decision.*
> **-CJ Calvert**

- **Accept personal responsibility for your future.** Perhaps other people have more free time, more energy, more skill, and more connections which allow them to accomplish things with greater ease than you. Agreed. So, once you've identified that... NOW WHAT? You still have to wake up tomorrow and live the life you've created through your decisions. Whining about the fact that you haven't got all the advantages afforded to others does nothing to move you forward, it merely leaves you sinking in a quagmire of self-pity. It isn't up to anyone else but you to make a masterpiece of your life. Most of the current quality of your life has come from past moments of decision like this: moments where you choose to do the great and difficult thing so that you could reap the reward in a future today... or moments where you choose the easy way out, ignoring the fact that this decision carries the heavy burden of living with the results.

ACTION STEPS

1. Decide what your big rocks are.
2. Build your schedule around your big rocks.
3. Focus on what today's most important task is, and resolve to do it first. How many minutes does it take before you take action? How many minutes can you stay focused on your #1 task?
4. Identify any time-wasting excuses you make and resolve to never again make use of this excuse
5. Identify any times that you are procrastinating on an important task. Why is this happening? Break the task down into smaller, bite-sized baby steps. Give yourself a reward for taking the first step, in order to overcome momentum. If a reward doesn't work, it's time to apply a little extra pressure and set a deadline with a consequence!

CHAPTER 4:

SETTING AND ACHIEVING GOALS

"The greatest achievement was at first and for a time a dream. The oak sleeps in the acorn; the bird waits in the egg; and in the highest vision of the soul a waking angel stirs. Your circumstances may be uncongenial, but they shall not long remain so when you perceive an Ideal and strive to reach it."
- James Allen

In March of 2003, while still working in my sales career, I was summoned to the office of our Global Director of Human Resources. Looking to move forward in my career, I had recently applied for a new position: to become the National Manager of Customer Service. But this HR Director had other plans for me. Along with the General Manager of Canada, they had decided that my skills might be more appropriate in a different role: that of North American Sales Manager for an elite portfolio of clients, called "Partners". I would drive the "Partner Program", it was explained to me. I would earn a fantastic income, have an incredible leadership role, fly all over North America (which was very exciting to me) and build our brand.

The meeting was going great, despite the fact that the Global HR Director was known to be, well, abrasive. However, he was being cordial and conversational for almost an hour, courting me for this role. Not only had I been hand-picked to do the job, he said, but they weren't even going to post the job on our company's Intranet; no other employee was going to get a crack at it. Everything sounded great until the Global HR Director casually added "Of course, CJ, you won't have time to do any of this "motivational speaking" stuff that you're so fond of; you'll be too busy."

It was an interesting moment, because my entire destiny was going to pivot in one direction or the other based on my next answer. Looking back, this moment was one of the top-five biggest turning points in my life. Without hesitating for an instant, I replied:

"Well then, I wish you the best of luck in finding another candidate for this job."

Dead silence. The Global HR Director was incredulous: he had spent an hour courting me, I had previously expressed my enthusiasm for the job, and all of a sudden I was getting cold feet? What on Earth was my hesitation, he wondered? I answered as simply as I could.

"Please understand, the job you are offering me sounds really exciting," I told him. "But it just isn't my DREAM. My dream is to stand on stage at convention centers with 10,000 people standing on their seats cheering. I want to *inspire* people. My dream is to be a motivational speaker."

Well, that was that. He coldly explained that I had until 12 noon the next day to make a formal decision, he dismissed me from his office, and as I was walking away he loudly called in his assistant to begin setting up alternative interviews. Over the next few months, my conversations with this man were… *tense*. He had a bad habit of regularly pushing people out of the organization. After being courted to be the North American Sales Manager, I tendered my resignation in October, 7 months after that pivotal meeting. I gave up the security of a paycheque forever, launched my speaking career full-time in 2004, and I have never looked back.

It's reasonable to think that most anyone else in the same position would have said "Yes" to the promotion. It was a HUGE promotion. It would have been a remarkable increase in my income. But I had a clear, driving, consuming GOAL. My point to you is that if you don't have a goal, you will be buffeted around by the wind. *Any* door that opens will look good. *Any* promotion will seem like the right choice. *Any* opportunity will look like the one at which to jump. But having a goal helps you cut through the fog. Because instead of getting a great promotion, you'll accept the RIGHT promotion. Instead of marrying a great person, you'll marry the RIGHT person. Instead of having a good life, you'll have the life of your dreams. In order to get what you want out of life, it starts simply with knowing exactly what you want. So, my question to you is: what do you want? If you've never set any goals for yourself, today is the day that all of that is going to change!

WHY SET GOALS?

"A soul without a high aim is like a ship without a rudder."
- Eileen Caddy

There is an urban myth about a Yale University study that asked students if they had any goals. As the story goes, only 3% of the students had written goals; 30 years later, the researchers purportedly returned to check up on the students and found that the 3% of the students who had written goals ended up having more wealth than the other 97% combined. Although the story cannot be corroborated, I have validated this principle countless times in my own life, and I've seen it work for hundreds of other people. People who set goals and write their goals down simply achieve more than the people who don't.

If we are going to do anything, we need to know the reason why. Let me share with you some of the top reasons why it is critical to set goals:

- **To accomplish results**
- **Goals motivate you**
- **You take personal responsibility for your life**
- **You get to see your future in advance**
- **Helps you make decisions faster**
- **They make you become a better person**
- **Goals force you to act according to your values**
- **Goals force you to keep score on your life.**

Goals help accomplish results. Most everyone dreams of wealth, success and happiness, and yet so few people seem to achieve what they desire. The truth is that a goal is more than a wish or a desire; a successful goal includes powerful ingredients to guarantee your ultimate victory. If you are going to get what you want out of life, you can't sit idly by and daydream; you've got to follow a plan to accomplish what you want. If you want your career to improve, you've got to define what "improve" means and you've got to create and follow your plan to make it come true. Goals deliver **results; daydreams simply deliver disappointment.**

> *Goals deliver results; daydreams simply deliver disappointment.*
> **- CJ Calvert**

Goals motivate you. When you leave the scene of a goal, you feel a sense of urgency and excitement. You are filled with thoughts of possibility. You can clearly see down the road, even if only for a minute, to the day when you accomplish the goal and you bask in the vision of how rewarding it will feel to finally cross the finish line. This excitement gives you extra bounce in your step, extra confidence in your spirit, and your mannerism starts to change. You go after opportunities with more assurance. You take action where you might have idled before. You get out of bed, excited to meet the day, because you have so much focus on the goal that you can't wait to achieve it! Life becomes exciting!

Goals force you to take personal responsibility for your life. Setting a goal says to the world *"I'm in a position of control. My good fortune is in my hands, not the hands of my neighbors or my parents or the government or my boss. I control my destiny."* Setting a goal requires boldness and courage, because it means you aren't willing to settle for your current accomplishments. You are striving to push yourself even farther ahead, which means you are leaving everything "average" behind. In fact, renowned leadership expert Orrin Woodward says "Setting a goal is a direct assault on the status quo."

> ***"Setting a goal is a direct assault on the status quo."***
> **- Orrin Woodward**

Goals let you see your future in advance. As you begin to flex and strengthen your goal-setting and goal-achieving muscles, you slowly build your belief about the efficacy of the strategies you're learning here. As you set goals in each area of your life and then enjoy checking them off your "To-Do" list, you'll start to realize that EVERY goal you dare to put down on paper starts to come true. This allows you to see your future in advance; you can predict the outcome of your life with certainty, since you know you are going to follow-through and create the results that you've envisioned.

Goals help you make decisions faster. When you are focused on a major goal and it is a driving priority in your life, it becomes very simple to make decisions about where to invest your time and money. With no overriding goal that directs your actions, you'll be tempted by anything that crosses your path: any other great-sounding opportunity, any other relationship, any fun diversion can easily derail you if you don't have a long-term focus. When you're faced with a choice between doing two different tasks, you won't suffer the discomfort of uncertainty; you'll know exactly which one to pick. You simply pick whichever task helps the greater goal. If one task helps achieve a minor goal, and another task will help accomplish a major goal, you go with the major-goal task. This doesn't necessarily mean work only; your major goal might be having a successful marriage. If a major business opportunity comes up on the night of your wedding anniversary and your spouse has worked all day on creating a romantic evening, you simply choose. Which goal is more important to you: The business deal, or your marriage? Knowing the hierarchy of your goals settles this contest quickly.

Goals make you become a better person. In the process of achieving a major goal, you will be pushed to perform at a higher level of operational efficiency.

You'll find out things about yourself that you never knew. You'll discover that you've got strength, courage, endurance, diplomacy, and talents that lay dormant until the situation demanded something extraordinary. At that moment, when the pressure is on, your genius is revealed. A major goal pushes you to your limits, and then past your limits so that they are reset forever. Every other obstacle you'll ever face will seem so small in comparison once you've accomplished a major goal. You'll be filled with a sense of self-esteem, a pride in a job well done, that you may not have ever felt before. Achieving the goal is remarkable, but the greatest reward you will receive is who you become in the process. As Mary Kay Ash says, **"A good goal is like a strenuous exercise -- it makes you stretch."**

Goals force you to act according to your values. Every goal you set will create a feeling of pride when you act to honor the promise to yourself, and cognitive dissonance if you act to betray your promise. Since you've asserted you want a result, you've laid yourself bare to the world and created massive pressure to take action, every step in the wrong direction will set off alarm bells in your head. Instead on munching on potato chips without giving it a thought, your subconscious will shout "Wait! You're on a diet!" If you've set the goal of saving money, every time you blow cash on unplanned purchases, your subconscious will shout "What about your retirement savings?!?!" If you follow all of the steps that I advocate, you'll tell everyone you know about the

> *"A good goal is like a strenuous exercise -- it makes you stretch."*
> **- Mary Kay Ash**

goal… and you might just feel guilty about letting them down.

Goals force you to keep score on your life. There is no avoiding the fact if you've missed a goal. A proper goal has a black-and-white finish line and you either complete your victory lap or you don't. You are forced to look above all of the minutia, distraction, and day-to-day noise that sucks average people in and causes them to lose years of their lives in aimless wandering. Most people are stuck on a treadmill, going nowhere fast, but because they aren't willing to be honest with themselves most people just stay on the same treadmill and keep running. Thoreau said "The mass of men lead lives of quiet desperation, and go to the grave with their song still in them." People secretly long for more, but they are unwilling to admit it to themselves. **Setting a goal is your personal admission that you desire promotion in life**.

Setting a goal is your personal admission that you desire promotion in life.
- CJ Calvert

POWER PRINCIPLES

"There is one quality which one must possess to win, and that is definiteness of purpose, the knowledge of what one wants, and a burning desire to possess it."
- Napoleon Hill

All successful people recognize that there is a simple formula in the attainment of their goals and dreams. These steps are so simple that many people mistake their simplicity as a sign of their redundancy. I couldn't disagree more: just because something is simple, doesn't mean it isn't critical. If you will follow these principles on faith, you will find that you attract a tidal wave of success into your life. If you doubt them, simply research the lives of successful men and women and you will find all of these principles hold true throughout their life stories. Follow the strategies they use, and you will reap equally powerful results! Here are the principles and strategies that I have used in my own life to create effective goals.

Effective Goals are Specific

"Our plans miscarry because they have no aim. When a man does not know what harbor he is making for, no wind is the right wind."
- Marcus Annaeus Seneca

A critical ingredient in the successful achievement of a goal is to first clearly outline what you plan to achieve. Without knowing what you want, you almost assure an outcome that is not aligned with your original wish. It's like going to the ticket counter at an airport and asking to buy a plane ticket. The first question asked of you will be *"Where would you like to go?"*

> *The exceptional man ensures that his goals are formidable in their specificity.*
> **- CJ Calvert**

Can you imagine answering by saying *"Oh, anywhere will do! Just sell me a ticket!"* Unfortunately, this is the exact strategy that most people apply to achievement in every area of their lives. And the results speak for themselves.

A vague goal leads to a vague plan of action (if a plan is even developed). A specific goal inspires a plan with concrete steps and a timetable of delivery. A vague or general goal is inherently weak. Murmuring "I'd like to be happy" or "I'd like to make more money" is the death-knell of purposeful achievement. Most goals that are idly wished for simply die on the alter of ambiguity.

The exceptional man ensures that his goals are formidable in their specificity. It is not enough to simply say "I want to be healthy." You must describe *specifically* what you want to improve. Perhaps you might say "I wish to improve my cardiovascular endurance and decrease my body fat percentage." Instead of saying "I want more money", say instead "I will generate $1,000,000 annual residual income from rental properties that I own." Now *that* is specific.

Effective Goals are Measurable

"The more specific and measurable your goal, the more quickly you will be able to identify, locate, create, and implement the use of the necessary resources for its achievement."
- Charles J. Givens

An effective goal is measurable. The reason this is important is because, if you can't measure the goal, you can't tell when you've achieved it. Without a clearly defined finish line you won't know when to stop running, and human nature suggests that most people will stop running well short of what they can or should produce.

For a goal to be measurable, it needs a quantifiable criteria attached to it. Basically, it helps to have some sort of number involved in the goal. For example, instead of saying "I want to earn more money" say "I will earn $250,000 this business year." Don't say "I'm going to lose weight", say "I'm going to lose 35 pounds of fat and gain 15 pounds of muscle, from my current starting point of 165 pounds total body weight".

Develop Milestones

With a quantifiable criteria attached, you are also able to break your goal down into milestones. If you want to write a 52,000 word book, you might set the sub-goal of writing 1000 words a week, every week, for one year. If you wish to save $12,000 this year, you may set the sub-goal of saving $1000 a month each month.

Milestones ensure progress according to your written plan and prevent procrastination. They ensure that the quality of your performance remains high because you don't leave the accomplishment of your goal to the last minute. They build confidence in your ability to complete the goal because you see small accomplishments building on your work as time goes on.

Effective Goals Have A Written Action-Plan

Your action plan will include the milestone baby-steps that you've just identified and preparation work for the task ahead. A complex goal will require a complex and highly-detailed action plan; a goal like "take out the garbage each Thursday" contains a written action plan simply by stating the goal! As you goal becomes more complex, you want to account for every variable and create a To-Do checklist to ensure you create results. Here are some key questions to ask yourself in developing your action plan:

- **What do I need to accomplish the goal?** (eg. time, money). What will the total cost of your goal be? If you are going to go to university, the cost of tuition is only one expense; you have to consider books, travel, living expenses, etc. If you are setting the goal of losing weight, what does the gym membership cost? Are you considering purchasing supplements like vitamins or protein powder? What about hiring a personal trainer? As well as the financial costs involved in your goal, you must consider the impact it will have on your schedule. How many hours each day or week will it require? What will you need to shuffle, delegate or delete from your schedule in order to make time to accomplish this new goal? In designing your goal, you need to be absolutely realistic about what resources are required. What if your goal requires more time and money than you have available? You will need to develop a plan to raise the money and find the time.

➢ **What skills or training will I require?** If you've never pursued a goal in this area before, you may consider seeking out an expert to help guide your way. What will you need to learn in order to achieve your goal? Are there any books that you should read?

➢ **What relationships will I require?** Are there any industry association meetings that will offer networking opportunities to move you towards your goal? Where can you go to connect with like-minded people who can open doors for you? Is there anyone who has experience in your chosen field that can mentor you and guide you through this process?

➢ **What are the obstacles I might face?** Start thinking about emergencies now, because they are bound to occur. Don't overextend yourself with time or money; plan on a few things going wrong.

> ➢ **What can I do to prepare for or prevent those obstacles?** Since obstacles are bound to arise, what can you do about them?

As you create answers for each of these questions, include this information in your action plan.

Effective Goals are Realistic

"The goal you set must be challenging. At the same time, it should be realistic and attainable, not impossible to reach. It should be challenging enough to make you stretch, but not so far that you break."
- Rick Hansen

Motivational speaker Les Brown says "If anyone has done it, it's possible that I can do it." This is a foundational belief of high achievers and one I would highly recommend that you adopt. Many people have an unrealistically low opinion of their ability to produce results. However, their lack of confidence dooms them to failure at the outset of their quest. But some individuals face a different challenge: they set goals that are not realistic for them to achieve. There are several reasons why a goal may be unrealistic. Let's take a look at them.

> *"If anyone has done it, it's possible that I can do it."*
> **- Les Brown**

First, the goal may be **physically impossible** according to current science. A person may wish to be able to fly and propose that they leap off a building to accomplish their goal. For the foreseeable future, this is absolutely impossible without the aid of technology (such as a hang-glider). A different example would be anything that stretches existing human abilities past their current known boundaries. For instance, swimming across the Pacific Ocean would seem impossible to most everyone. However, since humans can swim short distances, it becomes a matter of endurance and training before a person is able to accomplish such a feat. One day in the future, it *might* be possible to accomplish it.

Secondly, your goal might be unrealistic based upon **inadequate knowledge or experience**. You may dream of one day running a company. Maybe you want to write a symphony. Maybe you are newly divorced and want to start a new, healthy and lasting relationship. Are these goals possible? Certainly they are! But perhaps there is a massive gulf between where you are today and where you need to be in terms of your experience. Can you learn what is required of you? Most probably! The question becomes: what volume of information and experience must you acquire, what level of time and energy will you put into learning, how long will you require to learn it, and with that timetable can you still accomplish your goal in time? If your goal allows for a realistic amount of time to acquire the necessary knowledge and experience, you have eliminated one barrier to your success.

A third challenge is that you may have **conflicting demands on your resources**. For example, let's say you have a goal of getting night-time education at your local university. The class requires 2 nights a week, 3 hours a night. Is this possible? Certainly, as long as you are able to allocate that time. But if you also set the goal of spending more quality time with your family in that same timeframe, you now have goals that are fighting for the same resources. If you have a goal to save money, and you also have a goal to go on a vacation, if you are earning (and spending) the same amount of income, you now have a problem.

Fourth, **if your goal violates any of your values**, you will most assuredly sabotage your performance. If you enter a bodybuilding competition and you discover that the other athletes are using steroids, it might seem that the only way to win is to also use steroids. If your overall health and well-being are very important to you, then perhaps winning this contest is unrealistic and not worth pursuing. If you have a goal of being more adventurous and going skydiving, but value your safety above all else, the goal of skydiving might be unrealistic for you.

Finally, the goal is unrealistic **if you are unwilling to follow your action plan**. If you have a goal of saving $1000 a month, and the budget you have designed calls for a complete cessation of miscellaneous expenses, you might know that the goal is impossible if you are addicted to smoking a pack of cigarettes a day. If you have a fitness goal of losing 10 pounds in a month, and your plan requires 1 hours of cardio every day, you might already know that there is ZERO chance of you getting on the bike, let alone getting on a pedaling for one hour. In fact, the goal might be so big that the effort required just demoralizes you before you even start and you don't even try. You need to have enough self-awareness to know how motivated you are going to be, and set goals that push you past your comfort zone but are also challengingly realistic.

Effective Goals Have A Deadline

"When asked what he would do if he only had six months to live: Type faster."
- Science fiction novelist Isaac Asimov

A goal without a deadline is meaningless. Human nature being what it is, you are more likely to procrastinate than to accomplish. A speaker once said that **a goal is a dream with a deadline**. As I write these words, this book is scheduled to go to print in 7 days. Two days ago I firmed up my delivery date of the manuscript to the publishing company. I still have a tremendous amount of writing yet to finish! My father, upon hearing that I have only 7 days left, suggested that I delay the publication and take the time to really make sure the book was in tip-top shape before printing it. I thanked him for his advice, since it is reasonable advice, but I know the motivating power of a deadline.

> *I've never met a lazy person, but I've met lots of people who didn't face any deadlines with immediate consequences.*
> **- CJ Calvert**

If I continued to push the deadline back, the book would never be done. Since the only person I am accountable to on this project is me, I have to create an artificial emergency that motivates me: a deadline. The potential punishment: I'll send the book to print and it isn't ready. Because I don't want that to happen, I am highly motivated and effective at producing results right now. I have personally experienced the motivating power of a deadline on numerous occasions. In fact, I've never met a lazy person, but I've met lots of people who didn't face any deadlines with immediate consequences. People aren't lazy, they are just unmotivated, and a deadline with a consequence attached to it seems to do the trick for most people!

Effective Goals Are Written

"Write it down. Written goals have a way of transforming wishes into wants; cant's into cans; dreams into plans; and plans into reality. Don't just think it -- ink it!"
- Author Unknown

An effective goal must be written. Writing it down moves the goal from an amorphous concept and turns your goal into a concrete assertion. Putting pen to paper creates a contract with ourselves, and our conscience serves as the executor. Since our society places a high premium on written contracts over verbal agreements, our goals will carry a greater weight. By writing them down, we activate our subconscious by telling it "Pay attention. This isn't some common goal. This is something I'm serious about."

The dullest pencil is better than the sharpest memory, and by writing the goal down we preserve our moment of commitment in stone. We can no longer shrug off our personal responsibility to the goal by saying "I didn't mean it". On the contrary, you certainly did, at least in the moment you originally wrote the goal down. You can't come back later and play mental games with yourself. As well, preserving a bigger goal on paper is one way to prevent losing sight of those long-term dreams. It takes a tremendous amount of courage to admit a big goal even to ourselves, and if you aren't ready to act on a long-term goal today you at least keep a record of your dream for the day when you are prepared to act on it.

Effective Goals Command Our Focus

"Having conceived of his purpose, a man should mentally mark out a straight pathway to its achievement: looking neither to the right nor to the left, but straight."
- James Allen

If you are pursuing a massive goal, fraught with challenge and obstacles along the way, it is required of you that you focus on it daily. It must stir your passions when you awake and activate your dreams when you sleep. You must not be able to have a meaningful conversation without bringing it up. Your mind will be so attuned to the work at hand that you will see connections to your goal in people and in situations that had not been revealed to you before. It must be on the tip of you tongue and the edge of your thoughts. It is what you are about.

Focus is a tremendously powerful tool in our toolbox, and like all tools there is a proper time and place for it to be effective. In a toolbox, it's important to have a hammer and to have sandpaper. Both have a time and place, just as focus and balance have their own time and place. You will find you probably don't use the strategy of "balance" during the times that you are using the strategy of "focus". Usually, they contradict each other. But there are periods of time in life where the absolute correct tool to use is focus, and the correct thing to do is to neglect balance. For example, when our baby son was born, we were completely focused on him. There was zero balance. All other priorities were cancelled, delegated or ignored. And any parent can appreciate that this is the exact right thing to do.

Focus works best when it is followed by a period of rest and renewal. That's where balance comes in. By learning the appropriate times in life to use focus, and then switch to balance, you can get the greatest results. When you are called upon to exhibit focus, you want to ensure that this is a skill set in which you have great strength and ability.

The challenge for the majority of people is that, when they need to be focused, they are unable to channel their attentions on a single point. Instead, they diffuse their energies across a variety of areas, becoming a perpetual "Jack-of-all-trades, master of none". With focus, your actions will be concentrated like the rays of the sun into a powerful tool of energy that cuts a swath through the fog. Without focus, your energy will be diffused across the landscape of your dreams, never landing upon any single point and setting it ablaze. Just imagine the results you could create in your life if you would simply get serious and get focused on the thing that you want. The key to this is understanding the power of the words "Yes" and "No".

The word "yes" is equally a life-affirming and powerfully erosive word. 'Yes' can open the door to relationships, to adventure, and to opportunity. However, on the subject of FOCUS, the word 'yes' is typically flung about with careless abandon and shortsightedness. A careless 'yes' can erode your time, energy, opportunities, performance and therefore your results. The common man simply says "yes" to too many things. The exceptional man knows that focus is the ability to say "no" to every major goal but one.

So instead of saying "yes" to one goal, most people say yes to too many, drifting haphazardly between one goal to the next, never settling on a designated purpose and directing all of their energies towards it. The immature man seems to jump from one fad to the next, driven by peer pressure and unchecked emotion. The seasoned goal-achiever settles their mind upon the task and follows through with conviction. Just as a nail must remain unbending in its course to be effective, so too must an individual.

Just as a nail must remain unbending in its course to be effective, so too must an individual.
- CJ Calvert

BRAINSTORMING GOALS

"To dream anything that you want to dream, that is the beauty of the human mind. To do anything that you want to do, that is the strength of the human will. To trust yourself, to test your limits, that is the courage to succeed."
- Bernard Edmonds

It's time to have a little fun. For the next few minutes, I want you to imagine that anything you conceive of can and will come true. As Robert Schuller says, "What would you do if you knew you couldn't fail?" I'm going to encourage you to push aside any limiting thoughts, any negative self-talk, and any pessimistic feelings of fear or doubt. I'm going to encourage you to put your pen to paper and begin writing down exactly the life you'd like to have. I want you to think about every area of your life, not just your finances or health. What do you want to have? Where do you want to go? Who do you want to be? What do you want to accomplish? With so many examples of success that we can look to for inspiration, we truly see that the only limits to our future are the limits that are self-imposed.

> ***By writing your goals down, you are adding a little extra firepower against negativity, fear, and indecisiveness.***
> **- CJ Calvert**

I'm going to recommend that you also divide your goals according to time frame as well as category.

Think about what you want to achieve in the short-term, mid-term and long-term. Personally, I think of short-term goals as the next 90 days. Twelve weeks is enough time to transform your body, write a book, launch a business, buy a house and move into it, start a new career, take a course of study, and many other pursuits. Next, think about the next 3 years: where would you like to be financially, romantically, physically, emotionally? Finally, consider what your "life dreams" are; I would put these under the "long-term" category, up to 20 years to accomplish in some cases.

Don't stop writing until you've put everything down. Don't worry if you're not sure how you're going to accomplish something; this is just a brainstorming exercise. You aren't committing to accomplishing the goals you write down; you're just admitting to yourself what you'd like to accomplish if you had a magic Genie lamp with 3 wishes… or 3 dozen! Particularly with long-term goals, these are the biggest, most audacious, and perilously fragile. One word from a well-intentioned relative telling you how hard a goal is to accomplish, and most people give up on the goal without a second thought. By writing your goals down, you are adding a little extra firepower against negativity, fear, and indecisiveness. You can't come back later and say "I didn't mean it!" because, of course, you did mean it when you wrote the goal down!

Health. What sort of body do you want? How long do you want to live? How strong do you want to be?

What clothing size would you like to fit into? How often would you like to go to the gym? Is there a favorite sport that keeps you fit that you enjoy? How much energy do you want? Do you have any illness or pain from which you would like to be free? Would you like to be able to run a marathon, or compete in the Ironman?

Health Goals:
1-90 days: ______________________________
3-36 months: ______________________________
3 years+: ______________________________

Finances. How much money would you like to have in savings? If you have children, how much will their University cost for a 4-year program? When would you like to be debt-free, and how much will it take? When would you like to be mortgage-free? Would you like to carry around a wad of cash in your pocket at all times? Would you like a year of income saved in your "go-to-heck" account? How much money would you like to give to charity each year?

Finance Goals:
1-90 days: ______________________________
3-36 months: ______________________________
3 years+: ______________________________

Relationships. Who are the important people in your life? What can you do to invest in the relationships that matter most? What does your marriage need to take it to the next level? What can you do to make the time with your kids even more special? What about your extended family? How can you be a better friend?

Relationship Goals:	
1-90 days:	______________________
3-36 months:	______________________
3 years+:	______________________

Career. What would you like to improve about what you do? Do you want more leadership, creativity, opportunity to serve people, strategic planning opportunities, or charitable work? What amount of income would you like to receive? What hours would you like to work? Where would you like to be in your career in the next few years?

Career Goals:	
1-90 days:	______________________
3-36 months:	______________________
3 years+:	______________________

Emotions. How often do you feel stressed, frustrated, anxious, irritable, sad, worried, or discouraged? What emotions would you prefer to feel? Could you identify the people who, and situations that, are serving as triggers for these negative emotions and develop strategies to manage them? How would you like to feel? What emotions would you like to experience more often: joy, laughter, confidence, calm, or reassured?

Emotional Goals:	
1-90 days:	________________________
3-36 months:	________________________
3 years+:	________________________

Balance. What do you need to feel renewed, energized, refreshed and recharged? Do you like the thrill of adventure, or activities of serenity? If you had 4 hours to do anything fun, what would it be? Would you go rock-climbing, play Laser Tag, play softball… or would you read, garden or enjoy a hot bubble bath? What activities can you plan into your calendar to make sure you are taking care of yourself? What clubs or sports teams would you like to join each week? What VACATIONS would you like to take? What parts of the world would you like to see? What adventures would you like to embark on?

Balance Goals:	
1-90 days:	________________________
3-36 months:	________________________
3 years+:	________________________

Lifestyle. What sort of house would you like to live in? Where would it be? How big? How many rooms? Would any of the rooms have a special theme? Would you have a home theatre, a library, a reading room, a home gym, a music studio, an art studio, or anything else? How many cars would fit in the garage? What cars would you like to own? Would you have any other fun vehicles, like a jet ski, motorboat, or airplane? Would you have a closet filled with luxurious clothing and accessories, shoes and jewelry? Once everyone else is taken care of, why not have a little fun shopping! Think about some of the fun things you'd like to buy:

Lifestyle Goals:
1-90 days: ______________________________
3-36 months: ______________________________
3 years+: ______________________________

HOW TO MOTIVATE YOURSELF

"One of the strongest characteristics of genius is the power of lighting its own fire."
- John W. Foster

As we discussed in the previous chapter on time management, the way to motivate yourself to overcome procrastination is by using the power of rewards and consequences. With every goal you set, I'm going to encourage you to follow these key strategies to strengthen your personal motivation:

- **Write out a list of Pro's and Con's**. What is everything good that you will experience when you accomplish the goal, and what is everything negative that you will endure if you don't accomplish the goal? You want to lay all the information out on the table so that you clearly see the gravity of the decision you are making. Let's say, for example, that your goal is to exercise and lose weight. What are all of the positives that you will experience? I'd say you'll experience greater energy, heightened self-esteem for feeling proud that you followed through, you might feel more attractive, you'll have the body needed to enjoy life at the fullest, you will be able to be active later in life, your overall health will be greater, and you'll have the strength to do things that others may not be able to do. If you don't exercise, what are the potential consequences? You'll know that you let yourself down and didn't keep your promise, you won't be able to run next to your grandkids when they are riding their bike, you'll be huffing and puffing just to climb a flight of stairs, you'll put unnecessary strain on your heart with the extra weight you are carrying, you won't have the energy to live life the way you want, you won't be able to participate in every physical activity you might like to, and you may not live as long and healthy a life as possible. You want to create a long list of Pro's and Con's so that you get fully engaged mentally and sell out to accomplishing your goal.

- **Use Public Accountability**. Tell everyone in sight about your goal! And I mean everyone. Tell your family, friends, neighbors, co-workers, children's teachers, the gas station attendant, the kid at the Tim Horton's counter, the people on the elevator going up to work, the guy on the exercise bike next to you at the gym… everyone. Why on Earth would you do that? Because, by telling enough people, and telling them over and over, invariably people will start to ask you "How is it going?" Now you've got the added pressure of avoiding potential embarrassment. When many people know that you are pursuing a goal, every move you make in your environment is under public scrutiny. People become very aware of your daily habits and whether those habits are supporting your goal or NOT.

- **Set up rewards for accomplishing each milestone**. Sometimes, the intrinsic reward of hitting the goal is not exciting by itself. If this is the case, you need to make it even more pleasurable and exciting for yourself to follow through. Coincidentally, I don't need an additional reward to motivate me to write this book; just the thought of holding a published copy of the book in my hand is exciting enough to motivate me to follow through and do the work. However, I've got to be honest with you and say that many of the goals that I set are not as intrinsically exciting; many times I need to apply an additional external reward. If this is the case for you, just be honest and recognize it. I'd recommend that every time you hit a minor goal, you should reward yourself. The reward doesn't have to be something big; you could say *"I get to watch my favorite TV program when I do 30 minutes of cardio on my bike."* When you accomplish a goal, you want to reward yourself as quickly as possible, because it tells your brain that you get rewarded for doing the work. What I do is I see things in the mall that I like: a magazine, a CD, a piece of computer software. I purchase the reward, and then I put it on my desk facing me with a sticky note that names the goal I'm going after. I'm disciplined enough not to touch the reward until I've done the work, but what this does is it keeps me excited about doing the work. If the small reward doesn't work, just keep increasing the size of the reward until you are excited enough to take action and follow through on your commitment. If that still doesn't work, then…

- **Set up consequences for missing the goal**. People tend to run away from consequences faster than they run towards a reward. As I write this chapter, my coach and I have a friendly bet with a few of our exercise team mates: whichever team loses the greatest total percentage of body fat in a 6-week period, the losing team has to treat them to a steak dinner at the Keg. With this, we have several powerful motivators: the internal drive to "win" a contest and the disdain for "losing", the drive to enjoy a nice steak dinner, the pain of having to pay for someone's else's dinner... but most important, the potential pain of being the one guy who causes your team mates to lose. You see, if I don't get back to lean and trim in 6 weeks, not only do I have to pay, but my two team mates have to take cash out of their pocket and pay for dinner as well. I will actually cost other people money if I slack off, even if they do the hard work to lose the fat! THAT is some serious peer pressure! But that's exactly the sort of pressure that my team and I use to motivate ourselves to take action in every area: business, finance, fitness, relationships, everything. That's why everyone in our group consistently produces results in their lives: we hold each other accountable to success.

The Practical Application of Principles

In the spring of 2005, I was commissioned by an E.A.P. client to re-write their catalogue of wellness seminars. I had 15 weeks to write 15 1-hour presentations, along with facilitator guides, handouts and Power Points. This was a lot of writing and a grueling schedule. As a reward to myself for all of my hard work, I purchased a $1000 piece of music software (I am an avid music hobbyist and music composition is one of my great passions). The deadline I set for completing these seminars was Monday, August 15th, 2005. I purchased the software and had it sitting on my desk, *teasing* me, literally *beckoning* me to finish my work as quickly as possible. Well, August 15th came and went, and I was still working on the final seminar on Humour.

I had missed my goal. Clearly, the incredibly exciting reward (to me) of getting this music software was not enough motivation to compel me to attack my work with the necessary vigor. I decided to up the ante: I would switch tactics. Instead of using a reward, I would use a *consequence*. I re-set the deadline to Monday August 22nd, 2005 and decided that if I missed my deadline this time, I would literally give the software away. This would effectively be throwing away $1000 of my money; plus, I really wanted the software! Needless to say, at 3:00 am on Monday, August 22nd, 2005, I hit "Send" on my email and submitted the seminar to my client.

Here is another example. For years, I had neglected my music, instead solely focusing on my sales career. In January of 2003 I set the goal of building a home "project music studio" and beginning work on a new CD filled with instrumental music that I had been working on since high school. By Christmas of 2003 I had 4 songs recorded in demo version; by Christmas of 2004 I had 10 songs recorded in demo version. In 2005, I focused on writing the seminars for my client, as well as ghost-authoring a 69,000 word motivational book for another major client. The entire year was spent writing, with no time left for my music!

By March of 2006 I was feeling frustrated that this goal had been dragging on for several years.

I decided that I needed a firm deadline, and a firm consequence. The deadline was Christmas morning, 2006. The consequence: if I didn't deliver my finished CD (complete with professional photography on the insert, bar code, shrink-wrapped and ready to go on sale at the local music store) to my 4 best friends on Christmas morning, regardless of ANY explanation, I would have to take them all out to a $1000 steak dinner at an exclusive upscale steak restaurant in downtown Toronto called Harbor 60. Please understand that no excuse for failure would be tolerated: even if the CD manufacturing plant burned to the ground, if they didn't have the CD in their hands on Christmas morning 2006, I was treating them to dinner.

Well, my friends Steve, Kevin and Tom were very motivating. They would say things like "Hey, how is the CD coming? Are you falling behind schedule? Because, we're *really* hungry and we'd *love* a steak dinner!" This is what good friends are for: to keep you accountable!

In order to ensure that I hit my goal, I decided that I would submit my finished CD to the manufacturing plant on Monday, December 4th. That way, if there were any unexpected glitches on their end, the CD would still be finished on time. That raises a very good time-management point as well: create an artificial early deadline and leave yourself some buffer time for unexpected emergencies. That way, when the emergency does occur, you've planned on having extra time and you still deliver your work on the agreed date. I left for vacation with my wife, came back, picked up the CD's and proudly hand-delivered them to my friends the Saturday before Christmas.

ADVANCED STRATEGIES

"In this life we get only those things for which we hunt, for which we strive, and for which we are willing to sacrifice."
- George M. Adams

Here are the final tools I use to maximize my firepower when attacking a goal. Be warned: the use of these strategies may cause irrevocable positive transformation in your life and cause you to achieve at a higher level than you are previously accustomed. With practice, however, you can get used to winning with every goal you set.

Carry your written goals with you. My goals are in a plastic pouch in the front of my day planner, which I carry with me or keep it within reach at all times. Anytime I have a spare moment, I open up my day planner and review my goals for the year.

Review your goals on a daily basis. One of my professional associates in the United States built a seven-figure residual income in *4 months and 3 weeks* by focusing on his business goal every single night, watching motivational videos of other successful people every night before he went to sleep. In his timeless book, *Think and Grow Rich,* author Napoleon Hill says that you must "read your written statement [of your goal] aloud, twice daily, once before retiring at night, and once before arising in the morning." Every single day, review your goals so often you begin to dream about them!

Visualize yourself accomplishing the goal. Olympic athletes have crossed the finish line 1000 times in their imagination before they cross the finish line in the stadium. Since your subconscious cannot tell the difference between something real and something vividly imagined, make use of this powerful principle to pull you automatically towards success. Salim Khoja, owner of Power Within, graciously invited myself and my wife to enjoy the air show over Lake Ontario on his beautiful boat, *Motivated.* He shared with me the example of his own use of visualization to acquire this boat: he saw himself sitting at the helm of the boat, guiding it up to the dock, enjoying the feeling of the wind in his face. Powerful visualization will make use of all five senses; your imagination becomes more powerful when you touch, taste, smell, hear and feel yourself achieving the goal. Hear the roar of the crowd. See the flashbulbs of cameras going off in front of you. Hear your voice echoing out across the stadium and you offer your victory speech. If you can create a powerful image in your mind of victory, you are one step closer to achieving it.

Give a written copy of your goals to your team. Since 1995, I have given a written copy of my career goals to my mentor, Steve Stokl. Every January since 2003, I have given a written copy of *all* of my goals, personal and professional, to an even larger team of very special friends and coaches. As well as sharing my goals for the coming year, I also offer a final report on the previous year, citing which of my goals I did accomplish, and which ones I missed. Everyone gets a copy, including my wife!

Put a copy of your goals on the wall. When I am in the hot pursuit of a major goal, it gets posted on every flat surface in my home. I'm sure my wife loves how this improves our décor! But as I type this, I'm so proud of her that I see her own goals for her coaching website posted proudly beside the computer to remind her of her aspirations. I put my goals everywhere: on the fridge, on the front door, beside the computer, on the coffee table, on the TV stand, on the bathroom mirror. EVERYWHERE. That way, my environment helps keep me on track. Since willpower fades, you need to set up reminders that are independent of your mood or energy level. Physical reminders like this help me immensely.

Create a motivational environment. Pursuing and achieving a goal requires a lot of mental and emotional fortitude, and everyone requires an emotional recharge. As well as the positive energy I get from my mastermind association and my winning friends, I shape my environment to motivate me. In my alarm clock, I have a CD player that can wake me up to whatever motivational CD I'm currently enjoying. In my home, I love to put motivational sayings on the walls. "Successories" posters have always been a favorite of mine as well, as I find the photographic images evocative and equally motivating. I remember a guest coming to my apartment when I was 20 years old and the entire kitchen, floor to ceiling, was covered with either motivational quotes or pictures of the luxury lifestyle: cars, mansions, jets, yachts, etc. He couldn't believe it! He was stunned, because in his mind it wasn't "normal". Well, I'm NOT normal, and never want to be! High achievers don't live "normal" lives; their lives are *"EXCEPTIONAL"!*

Hang around high achievers. Tony Robbins says that "we rise to the level of expectation of our peer group." If our friends expect us to behave in a certain way, we will be pulled in that direction. It is almost impossible to overcome the power of association, so choose your friends wisely. I consciously choose to hang around people who are going places. I like high-energy, fast-moving, goal-achieving people. I truly don't even know how to have a conversation with someone who doesn't have some sort of goal in some area of their lives. The only thing left to talk about is the weather!

> *"We rise to the level of expectation of our peer group."*
> **- Tony Robbins**

One of my absolute favorite things in the world is to hear about someone's dreams and goals. I love to cheer for people! I love to know that someone is moving on! It is exhilarating for me! I hope that one day I get the chance to meet you, and that you feel comfortable coming up to me to share with me whatever goals you have.

Have a mastermind team. On a weekly basis, I meet with the people in my life who coach me on my fitness, finances, career… in fact, I'm blessed that my team has a lot of wisdom to share about every area of life! I have consciously sought-out and surrounded myself with high-achievers, but I have worked to formalize our regular meeting with an agenda to review our goals. As much as it is great to associate with winners, it's also important to have a meeting that you review your goals formally. This way, you separate socializing from coaching and you make sure that both get done. The members of my mastermind team have different areas of expertise, because it is rare that you will meet someone who is a genius at achieving as well as teaching each area of life. If someone is a superstar in one area, but less successful in another, I still want to hear their expertise in the area that they have flourished. I want to learn what worked for them, what didn't, and work to apply those success principles in my own life.

Be accountable. Meeting with high-achievers is a gift. But unless you take personal responsibility to stay in touch, the time you invested in the meeting would be wasted. Once you set a goal in a key area of your life, and you break the goal down into daily and weekly action steps, I believe it is incumbent upon you to stay in touch with your accountability team on a daily or weekly basis.

In my sales career, I phoned my great mentor Steve Stokl on a daily basis, leaving a voicemail to report everything that I had done correctly that day. The purpose of this was first, to give him enough information to guide me in the right direction for success, but also to highlight the days that I didn't do what I had promised. If Steve didn't hear from me, he automatically knew that I had slacked off and not kept my word to myself. I wasn't performing at the level to which I was capable of.

Immediate feedback keeps you on track on a daily basis and heightens your performance. Without it, most people succumb to weakness, temptation, fatigue, or distractions. By being accountable, you know that someone is watching. In the words of Dr Steve Stokl, "When you set a goal, tell three people whose love and respect is so important to you, that to let them down would be more painful than doing the work."

State your goals in a positive-tense. In writing the goal, it is important to state it in the positive tense. Saying "I DON'T want to eat junk food" is much less effective than saying "I want to eat nutritious food." The reason is because your brain doesn't recognize the words "don't want", it sees only the word "junk food" and gravitates towards that.

Identify the Daily Habits required of you. Every major goal should be broken down into bite-sized baby-steps. If possible, you want to reduce a goal to the daily steps that you must take in order to assure success. Always ask "What is required of me today to make my long-term goals come true?" Make a To-Do list of the daily

> *"The secret of your future is found in your daily routine... You will never change your life until you change something that you do daily."*
> *- Mike Murdock*

habits required to accomplish your long term goals in fitness, relationships, career, money and balance. Tackle this To-Do list with gusto. Mike Murdock says "The secret of your future is found in your daily routine... You will never change your life until you change something that you do *daily*."

In my sales career, I resolved that I would make 5 business contacts every day. If it was 3am, and I hadn't made the contact, my eyes would snap open in bed and I'd realize I hadn't done what I promised. Without any exaggeration, there have been many nights where I moaned with the realization that I had not completed that days work... and with great pain I rolled out of bed, put on my clothes, and headed out the door to cold-contact any human being who was awake at 3am. The point was not that I would get any sort of quality contact at that hour; the point was that it was incredibly inconvenient, bordering on painful, to drag myself out of bed.

Why on Earth would I do this to myself? Because the next day, groggy and uncomfortable from sleep deprivation, I wouldn't hesitate to make my mandatory 5 new business contacts. All of the fear, indecision and laziness were erased. I didn't care at all if the prospect wanted what I was selling; I just made the contacts to ensure that I wouldn't have to get out of bed at 3am that night! And, by tricking myself into taking action, invariably I made several good contacts in the process, even though I was forcing myself mechanically to just perform.

GOAL-SETTING WORKSHEET

Goal:

____

Deadline:

____

PREPARATION - Getting Ready

What do I need to accomplish the goal? (eg. time, money)

____

What skills or training will I require?

____

What relationships will I require?

____

What are the obstacles I might face?

____

What can I do to prepare for or prevent those obstacles?

____

ACTION PLAN - List the key tasks that must be accomplished

Tasks	**Deadline**	**Reward**
❑ ______________________	__________	_______
❑ ______________________	__________	_______
❑ ______________________	__________	_______
❑ ______________________	__________	_______
❑ ______________________	__________	_______
❑ ______________________	__________	_______
❑ ______________________	__________	_______
❑ ______________________	__________	_______

MOTIVATION

List the Pro's and Con's of accomplishing this goal:

Pro's: ____

Con's: ____

Who is on your Accountability Team:

____

What is the final reward for accomplishing this goal:

____

What is the consequence if you DON'T accomplish this goal:

____

CHAPTER 5:

OVERCOMING OBSTACLES

"It is defeat that turns bone to flint, and gristle to muscle, and makes people invincible, and formed those heroic natures that are now in ascendancy in the world. Do not, then, be afraid of defeat. You are never so near to victory as when defeated in a good cause."
– Henry Ward Beecher

In 1952, a then largely unknown mountaineer named Edmund Hillary attempted what seemed the impossible: to scale Mount Everest, the highest mountain then known to man. At 29,000 feet straight up, it represented an immovable pillar of failure for the majority of men who attempted to reach its apex, and certain death for some of those.

However, what is most interesting about Hillary is that in 1952, he failed. Only a few weeks would go by before he was asked to give a speech about his remarkable attempt. Everyone in the audience was awestruck by this man's courage and determination, but Edmund Hillary was seething with disappointment. When he took the stage, he pointed to a photograph of Mount Everest and famously shook his fist, shouting "*Mount Everest, you beat me the first time, but I'll beat you the next time because you've grown all you are going to grow... but I'm still growing!*"

> ***"Mount Everest, you beat me the first time, but I'll beat you the next time because you've grown all you are going to grow... but I'm still growing!"***
> **- Edmund Hillary**

On May 29, 1953, Edmund Hillary accomplished what he meant to do: he became the first human being to stand on the peak of Mount Everest. He was later knighted for his effort and will be remembered through history as Sir Edmund Hillary, a remarkable example of the power of persistence.

What Hillary recognized is what all persons of excellence discover: that all great adventures, all daring attempts to brave new frontiers and build new monuments will inevitably force one to face challenges that you could not have foreseen at the outset of your journey. It is in the endurance we display through the storms of our journeys that we distinguish ourselves as those who finish the race versus those who merely start. And our journey to success requires of us that we learn, change and grow to meet those unforeseen obstacles that invariably arise.

It takes courage to begin all great endeavors; it takes perseverance to complete them. And history makes little mention of the multitude of great and feeble attempts begun in the throes of initial excitement. The world only cares for the finished product. The 'might-have-been's', 'almost-done', 'came-so-close' and 'I did my best' stories earn their rightful place in the dust bin of obscurity.

When Napoleon was asked what the greatest quality of a soldier was, he did not answer 'courage'. He did not answer 'leadership'. He said, *'endurance'*. Endurance is the critical factor; the ability to carry on when others would flee, to press on when others are discouraged, to rise again when the will of others has been broken. To win a boxing match, you need only continue to get up off the mat, and make sure your opponent does not. To win at life, you need only get up every time you feel defeated. Motivational speaker Les Brown says *"When life knocks you down, try to land on your back... because if you can look up, you can get up! Land on your back!"*

> ***"It takes courage to begin all great endeavors; it takes perseverance to complete them."***
> - CJ Calvert

STRATEGIES TO OVERCOME OBSTACLES

"Here is the rule to remember in the future, When anything tempts you to be bitter: not, "This is a misfortune" but "To bear this worthily is good fortune."
- Marcus Aurelius

It is inevitable that some of the goals you set will not come to fruition. In fact, my personal opinion is that if you hit every goal you set, then your goals were too easy! It is only when you *miss* a goal that you discover what the limits of your ability are. You haven't aspired to great enough heights until you spend yourself in a worthy endeavor and come up short. The true champion constantly pushes themselves, sometimes over-reaching, but decides to reset the goal and try again. I've often missed goals, and had to set them again, sometimes for several *years*.

In fact, this book is a *perfect* example of overcoming obstacles and deciding to try again: I've reset the goal of writing this book every year for *three years*, started the book at least 3 times and discarded the work, had massive interruptions both positive and negative, literally had my computer crash and lost entire finished chapters, and finally decided enough was enough.

So, what goals have eluded you? Did you try to expand your business by making some new cold-contacts, but you fear rejection and you are avoiding picking up the phone? Are you trying to lose weight, but can't seem to "find the time" to exercise... or you keep eating junk food? Everyone has a story, and most of our stories are filled with examples of setbacks. But this entire chapter is about arming your mind with enough information to know that it's possible to break through your barriers and claim success, despite any setbacks you might have faced!

In order to prime your success pump, I'm going to share with you 7 principles you need to prepare to break through your obstacle. These are tools that I personally use, and each principle is a powerful weapon in your arsenal of success. Use them with caution: you might find yourself accomplishing every goal you set!

The strategies are:

1. **Fight Fear With Faith**
2. **The Door To Success Swings On The Tiny Hinges Of Discipline**
3. **Make The Decision... Once**
4. **Use The Tool Of Comparison**
5. **Keep Your Eyes On The Prize**
6. **Re-Fill Your Courage Tank**
7. **If You Can't Fight Back, At Least Keep Standing**

Fight Fear With Faith. Both fear and faith are birthed from the cradle of your imagination. Both of them are a projection of how you believe the future will unfold. The critical difference is that fear imagines the worst-case doomsday scenario, and faith imagines the greatest blessings possible. Both times you are engaging your creative faculties and bringing the full might of your imagination to bear on the task at hand; however, you need to take control of your thoughts. Be pragmatic: does fear serve to motivate you? If so, by all means use fear as a powerful tool in your arsenal. But if fear is paralyzing you and causing inactivity, you need to put fear aside and instead direct your thoughts towards a brighter outcome. Choose to see what positives can come out of a situation.

> *"Both fear and faith are birthed from the cradle of your imagination."*
> - CJ Calvert

The Door To Success Swings On The Tiny Hinges Of Discipline. Water slowly and imperceptibly erodes the rock until a small crack becomes the Grand Canyon. People who reach the finish line may not be the fastest, they are simply the most consistent. They realize that success is found in the tiny things we do every day, and they become masters of the fundamentals. When ever you reach a roadblock, go back to the basics and audit yourself: are you doing all of the small things correctly and consistently each day? Your consistent discipline will wear down the obstacle before you.

Make The Decision... Once. When you start and stop your effort, you lose all momentum. Consider the analogy of pushing a car up a hill. It takes an incredible amount of energy to get it going, but once you do it requires much less effort to keep it going. However, if you let up on your effort and the car slows down, you've got to repeat all of your previous exertions in order to get the car back to the momentum you had already built up. Once things are rolling, keep your foot on the gas peddle. Don't start and stop on your pursuit to success.

Use The Tool Of Comparison. Ask yourself if anyone else has ever encountered an obstacle of equal or greater size than the one you are facing. If you have lost your car, imagine someone who has lost their home. If you have lost your finger, imagine someone who has lost their legs. When we actively seek out examples of people in worse situations than we are in, it does two things: first, it reminds us that things aren't so bad, because they could be a whole lot worse. This allows us to enjoy a proper sense of gratitude for our blessings. Second, it may offer some powerful examples of inspiration: if someone who has lost their legs chooses to be cheerful and find ways to overcome their challenge, maybe we can too.

Keep Your Eyes On The Prize. Celebrated Pastor Mike Murdock says that "The reason most men fail is broken focus." It is very easy on the path to success to become distracted by minor obstacles. It is easy for most people to justify throwing in the towel when they face major obstacles. But the world has never been changed for the better by people who lost focus. It is always those brave and daring souls who recklessly plunge forward on their journey to success when defeat is snapping at their heels. Every day, remind yourself of why you get out of bed, the greater good

> *"The reason most men fail because of broken focus."*
> *- Mike Murdock*

that your life will serve, the impact you will make on the world and the lives around you.

Re-Fill Your Courage Tank. Discouragement literally means that we have lost courage. Understand that people who have courage are not necessarily devoid of fear. They simply act in spite of fear. They acted five minutes longer on the battlefield than someone who was gripped by fear. Look to examples in history of people who have thrown themselves out of the foxhole and raced up the hill towards the machine gun nest. Look to examples where people have risked their entire career and all of their wealth in order to stand against tyranny and do the right thing. If those people of history could do what they did, surely we can overcome our obstacles. With your heart pounding, hands shaking and sweaty, you simply need to force yourself to do what you know you must do. And amazingly, many times you will discover to your chagrin that the very thing that seemed so intimidating and overwhelming now seems so small and irrelevant. Most fears are entirely made up in our own minds, and deserve no attention. When you feel fear, it is a signal that you should prepare yourself to take action. It is an exciting feeling, because you are alive and well and in the pursuit of something that is clearly meaningful to you. It is a sign that you are living a life of purpose.

> *"Regroup, recharge, retaliate and rejoice."*
> *- CJ Calvert*

If You Can't Fight Back, At Least Keep Standing. In 1976, Mohammad Ali faced George Forman in a highly-promoted boxing match in Zaire, Africa. Ali, well past his prime as an aging athlete, was not favored to win against the formidable 26-year-old gladiator. When the match began, Foremen leapt out of his corner and began relentlessly pummeling Ali. It was all Ali could do not to hit the mat. The only thing he could do was literally stand still, keeping his gloves up, pressed up against the ropes, and absorbing as much of the assault as possible. Round after round, Foreman pushed Ali into the ropes and hammered on him. But after a few rounds, audience members started to notice that Foreman was fatiguing. His punches were landing with less force; the speed of his swing was fading; his face showed the weariness of exhaustion creeping in. And all along, Ali waited. Ali knew that he couldn't fight back against George Foreman's strength or speed, but he knew that eventually Foreman would tire out. And so, in the final rounds, as Foreman struggled to continue, Ali suddenly leaped off the ropes and pummeled him into the ground. This technique, called "Rope a Dope", helped Ali go home with the championship title once more. If you can't muster the strength to repel your opponents, just hang on long enough so that you can live to fight another day. **Regroup, recharge, retaliate, and rejoice**.

PRINCIPLES OF DETERMINATION

Never Yield To Discouragement

"I have learned that the harder the obstacles, the bigger the humiliation, and the greater the disappointments, then the larger the subsequent successes will be, as long as you learn and never give up. So now, failures will disappoint me, but they make me look forward to the future."
- Lloyd Lam

When Florence Chadwick first tried to swim the English Channel, which measures over 21 miles across, she came within 3 miles of the coast of France before quitting. Over 85% of the goal accomplished, and yet she threw in the towel. Why? At the time of her attempt, a thick fog had rolled in, obscuring her visibility. Although she could see the boats that were nearby to offer emergency assistance, she couldn't see the goal for which she was aiming. She no longer had the faith to believe that she could finish. She found herself growing exhausted and discouraged. And so, 3 miles from her goal, she quit. Afterward, she asked the crew how close she had come, and was amazed to learn what little relative distance remained on her journey. She commented that if she had only been able to see how close she was, she would never have quit.

Interestingly, this is not a unique response. Most well-intentioned people trying to better themselves and create a future will dare greatly and risk everything, only to quit within a few feet of the finish line. Why? *Most people do not realize how close they are to success.* With no clear end in site, the journey to success is exhausting to the hearts and minds of people, and discouragement wins the battle.

What is discouragement? Literally, you lose your courage. Faith wavers, hope falters, confidence fails, and you manifest your negative beliefs. If you only knew how close you were to completing your goal, you might attempt what you believe to be impossible.

Years ago, I came across a psychology study that showed the affects of encouragement in relation to completion of a goal. The subjects were asked to place their feet in freezing cold ice water, which was so uncomfortable as to border on being painful. Then, they were timed to see how long they could last before pulling their feet out. With no finish line to judge by, the first group of participants quit very quickly. The next group of participants were seated before the buckets of ice water and given the same instructions, with one crucial difference: they would have an assistant beside them with a stopwatch, cheering them on and advising them of their progress. As the seconds ticked by, the advisors would say "okay, you're at a minute; you've passed the time of the other group. You're doing great, keep going, you can hold on longer, 1:30, 2:00, 2:30…". It seemed almost magical to some onlookers, but the people who had someone encouraging them were able to last 3 times longer than the people who had no idea how close they were to success.

Keep Your Hopes Up

"The men whom I have seen succeed best in life always have been cheerful and hopeful men; who went about their business with a smile on their faces; and took the changes and chances of this mortal life like men; facing rough and smooth alike as it came."
- Charles Kingsley

A major component of persistence is the belief that you will eventually enjoy victory. The crushing blow comes when you don't think that you can make it: that the obstacles are too great, the odds against you are overwhelming; that you don't have the strength or energy to go on, and that the cost of continuing your quest is too painful. All of these issues stem from the underlying belief that you won't make it. The wounded warrior starts to picture a lifetime of futile struggle in search of an impossible treasure. Hope is your greatest ally in your journey and is the foundation of persistence.

How do you build hope when you've faced crushing setbacks? You must draw from examples of other men and women who have dared greatly and succeeded. Draw strength from the stories of their journey. Consider what you are attempting... has any human being ever done what you are trying to do?

> ***"Hope is your greatest ally in your journey and is the foundation of persistence."***
> **- CJ Calvert**

In 1954, the belief on the planet was that no one could run faster than a 4-minute mile. Doctors warned that it would cause a cardiac arrest in the athlete; scientists explained that the human body was incapable of such sustained exertion. And then along came Dr Roger Bannister, a 25-year-old physician at the University of Oxford. Roger Bannister had been training for months with his coach to develop his endurance with one singular goal in mind: to beat the 4-minute mile. And on that University race track in the summer of 1954, Roger Bannister shattered the 4 minute mile.

While this story is remarkable, what happened next is even more noteworthy. You see, up until that time it had never been done in the history of mankind, and yet as the weeks and months unfolded after Roger's historic record was set, several other athletes broke the 4-minute mile, and today thousands of people have joined the ranks of the 4-minute mile runners... including high-school students. What changed that allowed them to run faster than ever before? Were they eating a new type of food that gave them extra energy? Did gravity suddenly become lighter? Were they wearing a special type of Reebok running shoes? No; the only thing that changed was that these runners now BELIEVED it was possible. If it was possible for Roger, it was possible for them.

Character Growth Requires Challenge

"Character cannot be developed in ease and quiet. Only through experiences of trial and suffering can the soul be strengthened, vision cleared, ambition inspired and success achieved."
- Helen Keller

The Great Barrier Reef in Australia is world-renowned as the world's largest coral reef system, stretching over 2600 kilometers and visible from outer space. Vacationers from around the globe come to scuba dive, fish and enjoy one of the natural wonders of the world. But there are two sides to the Reef. The ocean-facing outer side is teeming with vibrant life and a flourishing ecosystem of coral and fish. The inland side is a barren wasteland with comparatively little activity. It is the ocean-facing outer side that endures and benefits from all of the challenge, and thus reaps the reward of growth. All growth comes through challenge; ease and comfort have never made any man a person worth remembering.

The process of muscle growth through physical exercise is analogous to the mental and emotional growth wrought through challenge: in order to grow, you must break down the old structure through terrible challenge in order that the new structure can handle a greater burden.

> *"We often don't realize it, but we frequently come face-to-face with the exact obstacle we need at just the right time to sharpen us where we need it the most."*
> **- Tommy Newbury**

Your talents are never revealed in times of peace; they are always tested and showcased during calamity. Anyone can coast and look good when things are easy. You find out who you really are when the roof caves in. Knowing this, would you not invite calculated hardship into your life with a sense of adventure? Realize that every setback you face is the doorway to promotion; in your job, your finance, and your marriage. As Tommy Newbury says: *"We often don't realize it, but we frequently come face-to-face with the exact obstacle we need at just the right time to sharpen us where we need it the most."*

When Enthusiasm Fades, Turn to DUTY

Perseverance to your cause and your stated mission in life is not necessarily "fun"; it is merely "right". All achievements are born in the daily discipline of the master who crafts them; when his competitors sleep, the master still toils away into the night.

When we have said that we will do something, we have staked our integrity upon accomplishing the goal. To attach your promise to a task is to measure your character by accomplishing the task. If you choose to quit, you've broken your promise. Who you are as a person is now in question. A promise does not allow for circumstance, distraction or setback. A promise does not include room for vacillation, for being wishy-washy and changing your tune when it suits you. Promises are not kept as a matter of convenience; they are kept as a matter of

> *"There are no hopeless situations; only men who have grown hopeless about them."*

honour. And making a promise that you will accomplish something says that you will, NO MATTER WHAT, finish the task you have started.

If you won't pursue the goal for yourself, do it for someone you love and respect, who would be disappointed in you if you fail. It's important to be at peace with the fact that not every challenge will offer an immediate victory for us. No matter how strong or capable, every one of us will face major defeats along the road to ultimate victory. The opportunity lies in trying to learn from our mistakes, to better ourselves, and return to the boxing ring with newfound vigor and confidence, a more capable competitor than before. What this means is that failure isn't failure until you've quit. Failure is a decision not to try again. There are no hopeless situations, only men who have grown hopeless about them.

GETTING UNSTUCK

"When nothing seems to help, I go look at a stonecutter hammering away at his rock perhaps a hundred times without as much as a crack showing in it. Yet at the hundred and first blow it will split in two, and I know it was not that blow that did it, but all that had gone before."
- Jacob Riis

If you get stuck, set ACTIVITY goals rather than RESULT goals. For example, if someone is trying to lose weight, many people look at the scale and get frustrated if their body weight doesn't decrease.

(This is a distraction anyway, since muscle is denser and heavier than fat... when people are trying to lose weight, usually what they are actually trying to do is lose FAT. A more accurate measurement would be someone's dress size or waist measurement.) Instead of looking at the scale, look at the actions you took today. Did you eat exactly what you were supposed to? If so, congratulations! Give yourself a reward! Did you exercise on your bike today? Excellent! Focus on activity goals. If your sales are down in your business, get out of a slump by going back to basics: track the number of cold calls you make, the number of sales appointments you arrange, the number of presentations you do, the number of clients that you close. Increase your activity, and the results will follow.

Still stuck? Reduce the size of the goal. Make a goal ridiculously small in order to overcome inertia. If one of my sales guys was getting cold feet about calling a client, I'd have him sit in front of the phone, pick it up and hold it to his ear. Not to dial the number, just to sit there holding the phone to his ear. Eventually, he'd start to feel silly and simply dial the number. If you need to get moving, break the goal into the smallest bite-sized step possible, a step that is so small it's easy to do, and you feel foolish not doing more. Trying to save money? Save a penny. Just one penny. Trying to exercise? Do one pushup; just one. You've overcome inertia, and you'll trick yourself into doing more activity.

If you miss a goal, try again. Many times in my life I have missed a deadline. However I do NOT miss goals; I just simply reset the goal and try again. I adjust my strategy until I achieve success. I have never handed in my goal sheet in January with every goal checked off. Every year, I must attempt some goals for the second time. Sometimes the third time! Just because you missed your target doesn't mean you've lost the war. Review what happened, what held you back, and how you need to grow as a person. What part of your strategy needs to be re-vamped?

If a goal no longer meets your values, you may choose to discard it. For example, from 1990-2000 I long had a goal of performing my symphony pieces with the Toronto Symphony Orchestra at Roy Thompson Hall. This is no longer a driving goal of mine; in fact, it's really only a "perhaps" goal at this point. The reason? It was a "means" goal, not an "end" goal. The end goal was that I wanted to hear my music performed, because I had only ever heard it on the piano and all of the symphony orchestration was solely in my own head. My ears had never enjoyed my own music, which was important to me. However, with the advent of more advanced computers and sophisticated music software, musicians can now compose and orchestrate entire symphonies in their computer. Thus, my actual goal of hearing my music has been accomplished.

However, there are several goals that I still have not yet accomplished in my life. One major life-goal is building and leading a positive organization of over 10,000 people that is dedicated to self-improvement, entrepreneurship and leadership principles. This has been a major life's dream of mine since I was 20. I have publicly stated this goal on my website so that in the years that I had struggled with focus, energy, and belief in my ability to accomplish this goal, the goal was still written down and I hold myself publicly accountable to accomplishing it. The reason I am writing of this goal here is to add extra pressure to myself to follow through with this long-term life's work. I attempted to achieve this goal in my 20's and failed. My promise to you is that I will succeed in this endeavor, and positively impact the lives of tens of thousands of people across North America!

OVERCOMING OBSTACLES WORKSHEET

What Goal are you struggling with?

____

List the barriers that have held you back and articulate them:

Barrier: **Describe the challenge:**

- ❑ Lack of Time ______________________
- ❑ Lack of Discipline ______________________
- ❑ Lack of Motivation ______________________
- ❑ Lack of Energy ______________________
- ❑ Lack of Courage ______________________
- ❑ Lack of Family Support ______________________
- ❑ Lack of Funds ______________________
- ❑ Lack of Skills/Experience ______________________
- ❑ Lack of Relationships ______________________

- ❑ Other ______________________________

Why does this barrier continue to challenge you?

____

What excuses are you mentally telling yourself about why you can't do this?

____

What do you need to change in order to accomplish the goal?

____

Who has overcome this challenge, and can you learn from them?

____

What are the consequences in your life if you don't succeed?

____

What are the incredible rewards you'll enjoy when you succeed?

____

What bite-sized baby-step can you take today to move you in the direction of success?

____

What reward can you give yourself for following correct daily habits for the next 7 days? (Don't worry about results; just focus on taking action.)

____

EXAMPLES OF PERSEVERANCE

"There is genius in persistence. It conquers all opposers. It gives confidence. It annihilates obstacles. Everybody believes in a determined man. People know that when he undertakes a thing, the battle is half won, for his rule is to accomplish whatever he sets out to do."
- Orison Swett Marden

Sometimes our own situation can feel hopeless; we've suffered so many setbacks, such crushing defeats, that victory seems like a pipe dream and failure feels assured. In those moments when we've lost belief, but we still hunger for success, we can look past ourselves and seek examples of perseverance that can inspire us. To know that lesser men and women have faced greater odds and overcome them can be the key ingredient to helping us stand and fight again. Here are examples of stories that have inspired me when I have faced my own defeats. Each of these stories helped me rise to fight again.

Harland's Recipe for Success

"It is by surmounting difficulties, not by sinking under them that we discover our fortitude."
- Hannah Webster Foster

History records the names of those individuals who dare greatly, who surmount seemingly impossible obstacles, and arrive on the other side of those battles victorious. However, for every story of conquest, there are a thousand other unknown stories of the almost-won, also-ran competitors who had the determination to start the race, but lacked the endurance to complete it.

Harland was a short-order cook who had struggled his entire life. His father passed away when he was only 5 years old, leaving him to fend for himself. He dropped out of high school at 16, married his sweetheart at 18, fathered a baby at 19 and divorced at 20. Already, the pressures and disappointments of life were piling up for Harland. He worked in a café, washing dishes and cooking until he retired at the age of 65. He received his first social security cheque for $105 and realized that he had to do something immediate and drastic in order to survive. He had no assets, no savings… the only thing he had was his personal recipe for seasoning and cooking chicken, a recipe that was a favorite of the regular patrons of his café. He borrowed a few dollars and decided to go on the road in an attempt to sell his chicken recipe. For the next few months, this white-haired, 65-year-old lived in the back of his beat-up car, traveling all over his state of Kentucky trying to sell his amazing recipe, only to face continued rejection.

At this point, most common men would give up. In fact, after the first restaurant saying "no", most people would simply return home with their tail between their legs, egos bruised and battered, and convince themselves that there was no point in trying. But not Harland. He believed that his chicken seasoning recipe was good, and that it would sell. So he received his first 20 rejections. And then 50. And then 100 rejections. Did he stop? No he did not. He did not stop at 240 rejections, 780 rejections, or even at a potentially crushing 1000 rejections. He kept knocking on doors, and on his 1009th presentation, he finally received his first "yes". Harland Sanders, retired short-order cook living in the back-seat of his car, would go on to become the multimillionaire founder of Kentucky Fried Chicken, one of the worlds most famous and successful fast-food franchises. What was his secret? PERSISTENCE.

So what is the secret formula that allows one man to dust himself off and rise again, when another man would succumb to defeat? Call it what you will: character, resolve, determination, or grit. In my mind, it's hunger; an insatiable hunger to accomplish the goal. I believe that the desire to win can supercede self-doubt. It can overcome fear. Hunger to win serves to motivate, to compel us to take action when naysayers have dismissed us and the bleachers are bereft of a cheering section to chant our names.

Winston Churchill

"We shall go on to the end. We shall fight in France, we shall fight with growing confidence and growing strength in the air, we shall defend our island, whatever the cost may be. We shall fight on the beaches, we shall fight on the landing grounds, we shall fight in the fields, and in the streets, we shall fight in the halls. We shall never surrender."
- Winston Churchill

Orrin Woodward, visionary leader and co-author of the New York Times bestseller *Launching A Leadership Revolution*, shared this remarkable story of Winston Churchill. He said of Winston Churchill that "his greatest achievement was his refusal to capitulate when defeat seemed imminent. One of Winston Churchill's speeches was worth an entire battalion of men. When the Nazi planes were bombing London, Winston Churchill would stand on top of the buildings and watch London burn. Hitler thought that by bombing London, he was bombing the people into subjugation. Winston Churchill knew that by bombing a free people, it only strengthened their will to resist."

His greatest known speech of all time also happened to be his shortest. Only a few years before his death, Churchill was invited to speak before his Alma Mater at their university commencement speech. He said: ***"Never give in. Never, never, never, never; in nothing great or small, large or petty. Never give in except to convictions of honor and good sense. Never yield to force, never yield to the apparently overwhelming might of the enemy. Never, never give in!"***

The Battle of Lake Erie

"Press on. Nothing in the world will take the place of persistence. Talent will not; nothing is more common than unsuccessful men with talent. Genius will not; unrewarded genius is almost a proverb. Education will not; the world is filled with educated derelicts. Persistence and determination alone are omnipotent."
- Calvin Coolidge

There will be times in our journey where the mountain pass has collapsed and seemingly insurmountable boulders lay before us. Part of persistence is the art of flexibility and creativity when faced with obstacles. "Finishers" are people who recognize that you may have to take another route to reach your final destination. When boulders clog the mountain pass, you have a choice to go over them, around them, or use dynamite to go through them. You must use good judgment to ascertain whether the obstacle is *impossible* to overcome, or simply *difficult* to overcome. It may be that an alternative route just isn't obvious at the moment. Just because you don't see an answer to your problems, doesn't mean that the answer isn't there; it may only mean that you have to be open to different solutions that you hadn't entertained.

Business leader and motivational speaker Chris Brady, co-author of "Launching a Leadership Revolution", tells a story about the Battle of Lake Erie during the war of 1812. In the midst of this incredible battle was a 27-year-old captain named Oliver Hazard Perry, commanding the USS Lawrence. He was stationed in the Great Lakes with the mandate to protect the waters and dispel British invaders. The Great Lakes region was strategically critical to influence over the Americas since travel by land was dangerous, pitting you against Indians, French trappers, British soldiers and lawless countrymen. Thus, whoever controlled the Great Lakes controlled the Western Theatre.

During the Battle of Lake Erie, the American fleet and the British fleet met. Aboard the USS

Lawrence, Captain Perry engaged the British ships and brought the brunt of his artillery against the British. However, he was outnumbered 5-to-1, and at one point in the battle he had all five British ships firing on him simultaneously. As his ship was being shot to pieces and his men dying around him, Perry was first stunned and then outraged to see that his American counterpart, the USS Niagara, has retreated to a safe distance outside of the range of fire. The cowardly captain of the Niagara, perhaps realizing that the odds against them were incredible, decided to hang back and let the battle play out... which would mean the end of the Lawrence and all of its crew. From its safe vantage point, the Niagara watched as the Lawrence was decimated.

From the mast of the "Lawrence" hung a flag that declared what is now a common motto in naval practice: "Don't give up the ship." Captain Perry, fighting for his life aboard the USS Lawrence, made an astounding decision at the height of battle. With 5 British ships tearing him to pieces and 80% of his men dead and dying, Perry gathered his few remaining men and descended in the last functioning lifeboat. They rowed furiously away from the British ships, which were now enjoying the leisurely sport of taking turns to try and blow the tiny lifeboat and its retreating captain out of the water. The British were amused with what they thought was cowardice of Captain Perry, who had "given up the ship" and abandoned the USS Lawrence. Perry and his men rowed as fast as they could toward the other American boat, the USS Niagara.

> *"Set your goals in stone and your plans in sand."*
> **- Chris Brady**

However, when Captain Perry arrived on the Niagara, the crew of that ship did not find a Captain who was retreating from the enemy out of cowardice. Blood-soaked and enraged, Perry leaped onto the USS Niagara and immediately assumed command of the ship. History does not record what the cowardly Captain of the USS Niagara said or did in those moments. But history does record that in moments after Perry's arrival on board, the ship was underway… turning directly towards the British ships and coming back at full speed to finish the fight. Perry was not retreating, he was re-arming! With a fresh load of cannon balls, a new ship and healthy crew, Perry raced back into battle and decimated the British ships.

In Chris Brady's words, this is an excellent example of "set your goals in stone and your plans in sand". While it would have been preferable not to "give up the ship", the plan needed to change in order to accomplish the goal. Captain Perry kept his eyes on the goal, and he accomplished his mission.

Other People Don't Define Your Future

Despite the belief to the contrary, the anonymous and faceless committee of "they" don't actually wield any physical power over your life and your decisions. However, if you let "them", "they" will wield incredible emotional control over your decisions and bend your actions to suit their whims. Never allow other people to direct your actions. Certainly seek counsel from the people who have achieved what you are seeking, but it is usually best to absolutely ignore the well-meaning friends, family, neighbors and colleagues who suggest that you not reach too high because you "might be disappointed".

Anyone who has ever achieved anything great has faced a long line of naysayers who tried to shoot down their dreams and cripple their ambitions. The names that we remember are those people who ignored the chorus of negativity and pressed on despite vocal opposition. Here are some examples of successful people who have faced rejection, and chosen to ignore the harsh words of their critics:

- R.H. Macy failed seven times before his store in New York caught on.
- Babe Ruth struck out 1,330 times, but he also hit 714 home runs.
- Woody Allen, went to New York University where he studied communication and film. Not being very committed to the program, he failed his film course and was eventually expelled from University. He went on to become one of the most celebrated film-makers in history, earning 21 Academy Award nominations and winning 3.
- In 1925, an aspiring actress named Lucille Ball enrolled in the John Murray Anderson School for the Dramatic Arts in New York. After only a few weeks at the school, Lucille was sent home in tears. Her teachers had told her that she "no future at all as a performer". She went

on to star in the hit show "I Love Lucy", and appeared on television for more than 30 years. She has received 13 Emmy Award nominations, more than any other person alive.

- In 1962, record executives at Decca Records auditioned a young group of 4 musicians from Liverpool, England. In a now-famous exchange, Decca Records turned the Beatles manager down flat, saying "Guitar groups are on the way out." The Beatles went on to become the #1 Rock band of all time.
- Thomas Edison found that his mind often wandered in school, causing his teacher to ridicule him and openly call him "addled". Young Edison lasted only three months getting formal education before he left to be home schooled by his mother. He went on to become one of the most prolific inventors of all time, creating the lightbulb, and being named by Life magazine as one of the 100 most important people in the last 1000 years.
- Ludwig Van Beethoven became deaf at the age of 46. Despite this, he was able to write some of his greatest works and symphonies in his later years, despite his deafness.
- Franklin Roosevelt was a four-term President of the United States, and was also crippled from the waist down. Having contracted a debilitating bout of polio while on vacation in 1921, he still managed to become Governor of New York in 1929, took action against the Depression with his "New Deal" in 1933, and come to the aid of Winston Churchill in World

War II after the devastating attack on Pearl Harbor… all from the seat of a wheelchair.

- Michael Jordan, heralded as the greatest basketball player of all time, was cut from his high school basketball team. At 5 feet 11 inches he was deemed "too short". His coach, sensing his drive and tenacity, offered to coach him over the summer and bring his game up. Simultaneously, he grew 4 inches that summer, made the team next year, and went on to lead the Chicago Bulls basketball team to victory many times over.

Get Back Up When You're Knocked Down

"Our greatest glory is not in never falling, but in rising every time we fall."
- Confucius

In May of 1992, while preparing for her Olympic race that summer, Canadian rower Silken Laumann faced a massive setback. While training, a German team accidentally crashed their boat in the side of hers. The accident badly smashed Silken's leg and she looked down through the gore of the muscle hanging by her ankle, and the bone of her leg clearly visible. With only three months to go before the summer Olympics commenced, her doctors told her that she would need to withdraw from the Olympics and give up on her dream of claiming a medal. With only a few weeks to spare before the Olympics, Silken gingerly attempted to recuperate. She was back in the water in

June, only a few weeks after her devastating injury, and she rowed right into the history books by claiming a bronze medal in rowing that summer!

What we learn from her example is that even when the odds seem against us, it always behooves our cause to stand and try again. If we don't try, we guarantee our failure. Wayne Gretsky says *"We miss 100% of the shots we don't take."* If we at least attempt to stand and fight again, at least there is a possibility of success. But without even trying, we doom ourselves to certain failure.

> ***"We miss 100% of the shots we don't take."***
> **- Wayne Gretsky**

Dreamers Can Face Violent Opposition

"Every truth passes through three stages before it is recognized. In the first it is ridiculed, in the second it is opposed, in the third it is regarded as self evident."
- Arthur Schopenhauer

In 1847, a Hungarian physician named Ignaz Semmelweis noticed a disturbing trend. A shocking number of new mothers, having just given birth, were succumbing to a violent fever and even dying. At this time in history, there was no popular theory of germs and therefore no understanding of how germs could be spread from a contaminated patient to a healthy one. Because of this, we could forgive the ignorance of well-intentioned medical interns who worked in the mornings performing autopsies, and then helped deliver babies in the afternoon in the maternity ward. This would be fine, except for the fact that the interns failed to wash their hands between handling the dead bodies and handling the new mothers.

Semmelweis noticed this trend and realized that there must be a connection between the morgue and the maternity ward. He surmised that the blood from the cadavers somehow carried disease that, when the surgeons touched the mothers during childbirth, the deadly disease was introduced into them and would subsequently cause their death. He postulated that if interns would clean their hands between tasks, using a simple formula of chlorinated lime, the mortality rate would drop. He tested his hypothesis by directing interns to clean their hands, and he was proved correct. The mortality rate plummeted instantly. But, because there was no overriding theory explaining why it worked, his hypothesis was received with disdain and was soundly ridiculed. He was ignored or harassed by the entire medical community, eventually losing his job at the hospital and leaving Budapest for good.

Semmelweis continued his assault against the status quo, writing impassioned letters to anyone in the medical community who would listen. People came to believe that he had lost his mind, and he was placed into a mental institution in 1865. Of course, Semmelweis was right all along, as history has proven. Later, the famous Louis Pasteur would popularize the germ theory of disease, which supported all of Semmelweis' findings and heralding him as the

> ***"People of integrity expect to be believed, and when they are not, they simply let time prove them right." - Scott Michael***

pioneer of antiseptic procedures. Sadly, Semmelweis did not live to see the world change its mind about him and his theory.

We might take from the tragic story of Dr Semmelweis that it isn't worth it to stand for your ideals and champion a just cause, because there is always a chance that you will face violent opposition to your ideals. Martin Luther King Jr. learned this fact. As did Abraham Lincoln, Mahatma Gandhi, and Bobby Kennedy. In 2008 we've seen the political assassination of Benazir Bhutto, the first female Prime Minister of Pakistan. All of these people staked their lives on an ideal, and their bravery helped serve to move the world one step closer towards its potential. The bravery of the few paves the way for the safety and comfort of the masses. I say to you that in order to live an exceptional life, you MUST make a stand on issues of consequence and conscience. We must always make the *right* choice, even when it is the *difficult* choice. If we have to choose between keeping our job and breaking the law, I recommend that you choose to leave an unscrupulous employer. If you have the choice between claiming credit for someone else's work or admitting that you didn't finish your own work on time, always own up to your mistakes.

To be very realistic, it is highly unlikely that you or I will ever face the threat of political assassination. It is more likely that if we take a stand on an important matter, that we will face opposition from friends, family or colleagues. Even if you are ridiculed, do the right thing. Even if you are opposed, stand for the right thing. Even if your good name is besmirched by false scandal, say the right thing. In the end, people of integrity expect to be believed, and when they are not, they simply let time prove them right.

ACTION STEPS

1. Identify a major goal you would like to accomplish. What obstacles stand between you and success? List each one of them, and develop a written plan to overcome each and every obstacle. Research the lives of people who have accomplished the goal you seek and the obstacles you must overcome, and learn from their experience.
2. Manage your positive thinking. People mentally talk themselves out of success before the world physically stops them. Our pessimistic attitude can be our own worst obstacle when pursuing success. What words do we say to ourselves? Do we think of the reasons why something won't work, or focus on all the reasons why it can, will and must? Choose your mindset and you choose your future.
3. Associate with winners. People who throw in the towel at the first sign of challenge aren't going to be good mentors for you along your journey. Hang around people who have the mental toughness, courageous heart and winner's mindset to see themselves through the tough times. Association slowly and subtly

shapes our belief system for better or worse; choose courageous friends and you will move towards being more courageous.

4. Draw strength from past victories. What obstacles have you overcome before? What enemies have you surmounted? Surely you've gone through some tough times… how did you get through them? Always remember that if you've faced some real challenges, you are stronger and more prepared for battle the next time.

CHAPTER 6:

SHAPING YOUR BODY

"I hated every minute of training, but I said, "Don't quit. Suffer now and live the rest of your life as a champion."
- Muhammad Ali

On August 11th, 2004, I made the decision to transform my physique forever. You see, up to that point I had never weighed more than 130lbs. I stand 5′8″ tall, and I've always had a slight build. In high school I was the kid who was small enough to push into a locker without fear of reproach. A strong gust of wind would have knocked me down! I felt that being so thin sapped power from my spirit since my physique was so clearly lacking in power. I wanted to change that.

The barrier that I faced was two-fold: first of all, there was almost zero information on how to go from being skinny to being big. When I say big, I'm referring to adding more lean muscle mass; I had no desire to "Super-Size" my way to 220 pounds and have a heart attack. But almost all of the exercise and diet literature is focused on either burning fat (and then subsequently sacrificing much-needed muscle), or becoming an Arnold Schwarzenegger-sized steroid-drenched behemoth. Neither of these alternatives were what I was after.

I had even made a bet in 2003 with a few work colleagues, and the bet was to see who would change their body mass by the greatest percentage. They were trying to lose weight, and I was trying to gain weight. All 4 of us threw $50 in the pot, and the 90-day challenge was on. Ninety days later, all of us quietly took our cash out of the pot and had an unspoken agreement to never mention the bet… because we were all mortified that none of us had made any progress at all!

My Secret Weapon: Tom Kiatipis

Everything changed for me on August 11th, 2004. I had seen a Canadian Bodybuilding champion and fitness coach named Tom Kiatipis deliver a presentation on diet and exercise. Tom has been featured in Canadian Living magazine, has spoken on stage for the Learning Annex, was named the top Athlete of the Year at Neutron Sports (the premiere natural bodybuilding organization in Canada) and will be leading the Canadian team of professional bodybuilders with Neutron Sports to compete internationally next year. He is a champion in everything he does.

I arranged to meet Tom at his home gym where he trained his fitness clients. We sat down at the desk he asked me what my goals were, what my motivation was, what I thought my roadblocks were, and he started to help me design a meal plan tailored to CJ Calvert. After an hour, he handed me a protein bar to eat, and it took me 15 minutes to painfully and slowly chew and swallow the bar. The reason? I never ate anything! It was no surprise that I was so skinny because I had such a small stomach and small appetite that it was impossible to make progress!

Over the next 12 weeks, Tom and I got to work on breaking through all of my roadblocks, redesigning my diet, and building a brand-new CJ. 90 days later, on November 12th, I had packed on 27lbs of muscle and dropped to 6% body fat. By March of 2005, I weighed in at 163lbs and had dropped to 4.6% body fat. I continued to maintain this weight until this last year when Tom and I decided it was time to raise the bar.

Even though I had enjoyed some huge gains, I had stopped improving and was sitting on my laurels. I needed something dramatic to motivate me to go to the next level.

We agreed that I would compete on stage in my first live bodybuilding contest, I initiated a year of focused effort, despite some big life changes like starting a family and renovating our new home. On May 3rd 2008 I stood on stage at Toronto's York University and took 3rd place in an Ontario-wide bodybuilding contest, the www.idfa.ca. I came in at 2.98% body fat on competition day. I am incredibly proud of my accomplishment, but please understand that I never made any improvements until I received proper coaching from Tom.

This raises an important point: most people continue to follow the same program over and over, and they yield the same results. If you aren't getting the results you want in fitness (or in any other area of life) **please stop taking your own advice**. My suggestion is to humble yourself, and seek advice from someone who has actually accomplished what you want to accomplish. It is insanity to continue to repeat a losing strategy over and over, and yet expect a different outcome. Take advice from successful people.

> *If you aren't getting the results you want... please stop taking your own advice!*
> **-CJ Calvert**

Over the next few pages, I am going to share with you some of the fundamental strategies that Tom has taught me along the journey of my own physical transformation. This information does not replace the need for one-on-one coaching (although I will talk later about the potential pitfalls of hiring many personal coaches at gyms), but I hope that this information serves as a starting point and a source of inspiration for you to begin your own physical transformation. Here we go!

YOUR MENTAL GAME

Make the Decision to Change

"Take care of your body. It's the only place you have to live."
- Jim Rohn

Your destiny is shaped in the moments of decision. When you decide to shape your body into the ideal level of strength, energy, muscle mass and body fat percentage, you will take action. Action is the residual proof left behind in the passing wake of a decision. You must choose energy over fatigue. You must choose fitness over infirmity. You must choose strength over frailty, health over illness, and longevity over burnout. You need to look in the mirror and take an honest look at who you have been. Since your body is the vehicle that you use to travel through life, how have you been treating your vehicle? The Bible says that the body is a temple. Are you respecting your body and honouring yourself?

> ***Action is the residual proof left behind in the passing wake of a decision.***
> **-CJ Calvert**

Sometimes we need to use fear to motivate ourselves to make the ultimate decision to change. A great question to ask yourself is "What will happen if I DON'T change?" Will things get better... or worse? Will you live long enough to see your kids grow old, get married, and enjoy your grandchildren? Will you have the energy to run beside your kids while they learn to ride a bike? Are you strong enough to protect your family? Are you healthy enough to continue providing for your family? There are a lot of people whom you love who are counting on your continued good health with their very lives.

Now, here is a more exciting question: "How good will it feel when you have the body of your dreams?" Do you want to get up in the morning and feel more energy coursing through your body? Do you want to feel strong and powerful? Do you want the confidence to know that you're taking care of yourself and you're going to last a long, long time? How proud will you be with yourself when you look in the mirror and know that you've finally done it; you broke through all of the excuses and just simply did what you told everyone you would. How great will it feel to slip into that bathing suit and show the world how dedicated you were? How great will it feel to reach retirement and have the health and energy to really enjoy life? You see, it all comes down to figuring out your reasons and making the decision.

When you decide to change, all manner of resources will become available to you. Making a decision fills you with confidence. It stakes your claim in the ground to say "This is what I am committed to." It energizes you and drives you towards your goal. It mobilizes you to follow through with your plans. It ensures eventual victory, since you've made a decision to win. When you decide to get fit, you're halfway to your goal!

Get Over Your Excuses

"In order to change we must be sick and tired of being sick and tired."
-Author Unknown

The number-one *verbal* reason that people offer me as to why they have not mastered their physical body is **"I don't have TIME"**. *This is utter rubbish.* Everyone alive has time for something; you're just giving your time to something else. Not to put the point too plainly, if you own a television and have seen it for a minute this week, you have time. The only people who don't actually have time to exercise are people who currently face absolute catastrophe in their lives; they are either working 16-20 hours a day at their job and literally collapse in bed when they get home, or they are racing back and forth from work to the hospital to sit at the bedside of a family member who is facing a medical crisis.

If anything is happening in your life that is as dramatic as the examples that I've just offered, then you don't have time. For example, when my wife went into labour a month early, I was sleeping on the couch at the hospital for the better part of a week while we were going on 1 hour of sleep at a time feeding our little premature baby. I didn't exercise for the two weeks after his unexpected and dramatic birth. When I had emergency surgery to remove my appendix, and couldn't walk for a week, I didn't exercise.

However, most people have lots of available time. **The first real reason that people don't exercise is because there is *no immediate consequence* to not doing it**. There is no motivation to take action! I might go so far to say that people are lazy, but that is not always accurate; often they are just unmotivated. Every human being becomes very motivated when the reward or the consequences are big enough. People simply don't exercise because the consequence of not exercising won't be felt for years or even decades. If you don't exercise today, NOTHING bad will happen! But 20 years of avoiding exercise will create a physical health disaster. If people knew they'd have a heart attack tomorrow, they would exercise today.

The second reason is *fatigue*. People are just too tired to exercise! Vince Lombardi says *"Fatigue makes cowards of us all."* Being tired is understandable, but it is not a valid reason to slack off. As well, if you are chronically fatigued, you need to identify the reasons for this and immediately take action to counteract them. Usually, diet, exercise and sleep habits are contributing factors to fatigue. Additionally, mental and emotional stress can be incredibly physically draining.

The third reason is *lack of belief*. People don't think it will work, because they've tried before and failed, so they don't want to bother! If you are convinced that your time will be wasted by trying, it's no surprise that you lack the motivation to get up off of the couch. Feeling hopeless about a situation doesn't make exercise look like a doorway to a better life; it makes exercise look like pointless work that might as well be avoided for something more important.

So, what's your excuse? It's too rainy out? You don't own the right running shoes? You'll start tomorrow? You DESERVE to enjoy all the great food at Christmas and you'll start dieting in the New Year? You don't have the willpower? You'll have to buy a new wardrobe for your fit body and clothes are too expensive? Understand that whatever excuse you offer up to yourself, it had better sound good, because it has to last you for the rest of your life. It had better sound good when you're sitting across from the doctor in a few years and she's giving you bad news; just remind yourself of the excuse then. Unfortunately, in that really terrible moment, I don't think that you're going to find a lot of comfort in the excuse you've been selling yourself.

> *"Fatigue makes cowards of us all."*
> **- Vince Lombardi**

Instead, why don't you change gears and make a decision to take action? So many people have done it. So many people who have bigger obstacles in their lives have put one foot in front of the other and conquered this "mountain" called fitness. If they can do it, surely you can too!

Make It A Priority

"When it comes to eating right and exercising, there is no "I'll start tomorrow." Tomorrow is disease."
- V.L. Allineare

Once you've identified the mental barrier that has been holding you back, and you've decided that you aren't going to be held hostage by that mental barrier any more, now it's time to take action. The only way I can guarantee that you're going to exercise is if you take action and make exercise a priority.

> *Exercise whenever you are willing to do so. It matters more* that *you do it, than it matters* when *you do it.*

It's pretty easy for me to say the words "make exercise a priority". What does that mean, exactly? It means that exercise is *important,* more important that almost anything. It means that when you make your daily, minute-by-minute decisions about how to invest your time, exercise is the option that comes to mind first. It means that when you have a choice of exercising or doing something else, you CHOOSE exercise before all other options! You may even want to identify a task or activity that regularly takes up some of your time throughout the week, and simply cancel that activity entirely so that you can replace it with a few focused minutes of exercise.

If you really want to guarantee success, exercise first thing in the morning if possible. That way, you can go through the whole day knowing that you've already accomplished your #1 priority! However, you may not be a morning person. Some people ask me

"Should I exercise in the morning or at night?" I am a pragmatic person, and I'm focused on results. My answer is always ***"Exercise whenever you are willing to do so. It matters more* that *you do it, than it matters* when *you do it. If it means doing it at night, exercise at night."***

Take Action NOW

"Initiative is doing the right thing without being told."
- Victor Hugo

"Well begun is half done."
- Aristotle

Don't wait for things to be perfect before you start your journey, because things will NEVER be perfect. There will NEVER be a day that you don't have something else that is distracting you. Nobody who becomes a champion in anything did it when things were easy and the journey was uneventful. You can't plan a road trip and wait for all of the lights to turn green, and all of the construction to stop, and all of the potholes to be mended. Life doesn't work that way. You have to do the best with what you've got.

So don't wait until you've got your entire meal plan written out for a week to decide not to eat those potato chips. Don't wait to learn how to use every piece of equipment at the gym; go ahead and use what you are familiar with. Do something! Put your shoes on and go for a walk. Drive down to your local gym and get a tour. Make the courageous leap and sign up for a membership. Pick up a copy of a great fitness book like "Body for Life" at your local bookstore and begin mastering the fundamentals of fitness. Read, learn and prosper in your journey towards personal excellence. Charles Schwab said *"The best place to succeed is where you are with what you have."*

In the beginning, set activity goals; do NOT set result goals. What is a result goal? When you hop on the scale and pray that the number has gone down after being on the treadmill for 1 day. Stop looking at your results in the beginning; it's just discouraging and it's not realistic. The goal you should be attempting to achieve is the goal of changing your lifestyle and daily habits. If you do this, everything else will take care of itself. Daily habits yield massive and powerful results. Congratulate and reward yourself when you do the right things each day, and stop knocking yourself if you don't see immediate progress.

> ***"The best place to succeed is where you are with what you have."***
> **- Charles Schwab**

THE WINNING STRATEGIES

Improve Your Numbers

"Never mind what others do; do better than yourself, beat your own record each and everyday, and you are a success."
- William Boetcker

When I was 15 I got my first set of weights. I got Arnold Schwarzenegger's manual on working out, wrote out his program on a piece of paper, and started exercising. His program was fantastic! Some of these exercises I'd never been exposed to, and I saw immediate and massive results. The problem was that I had a book coaching me, just as this book is coaching you now. A book cannot be your coach; it can only be your starting point. As well-intentioned and experienced any author might be (including myself), I don't know your body type, strength level, whether you have injuries, your age, your current intake of protein and carbs, or any other factor that can dramatically affect your performance and ability to get results in the gym. So I'm going to share a secret that will enable you to coach yourself. The secret is: **beat your numbers, every time!**

The purpose of exercise with weights is to build muscle mass and strength. The way that this occurs is that you actually lift the weights with a goal of slightly damaging the muscles. Lifting weights causes microscopic tears in your muscles fibers. Through this strategic injury, your muscles heal and acclimate to the damage done. When they heal, they are larger and stronger. The process of forcing them to adapt to the demands that you put on them is called resistance training.

Every time you exercise any muscle, the goal should be to increase the number of times you can lift the weight (called repetitions or 'reps' for short) or the amount of weight you are lifting. For example, if you do 10 bench-presses, you should set the goal the next time you work out of lifting the weight 11 times or more if possible. Once you reach a certain number, say 12 reps, for reasons I will explain below you will want to increase the weight. So, lets say you are bench pressing 250lbs; you may want to increase the weight to 260lbs or 270lbs. This will cause the number of reps you can do to decrease, perhaps to 8 reps. Then, you want to work back up to being able to do 12 reps, and repeat the process. Increase the weight slightly, get back up to 12, and so forth.

Use some strategy with the amount of weight you increase. You don't want to add so much that you can only do 1 or 2 reps, you want to keep your rep range between 8-12 (explained later in this chapter). So, if you're lifting 100lbs, don't go up to 200. If you're lifting 50lbs, you may only want to increase to 55lbs. If you are lifting 10lbs on a lateral raise, you may only want to go up to 12lbs. Keep in mind the percentage increase, not just the numerical value of the weight. If you are leg pressing 400lbs, you may want to go up to 450lbs.

Track Your Numbers

Most of the time, I work out in the personal home gym of my fitness trainer and best friend, Tom Kiatipis. Tom has invested in all of the advanced equipment found at any public gym in order to shape his body into a trophy-winning machine, so we've got everything we need to stay fit and bring home medals when we compete. On the times I go out to a public gym where I have a membership, I am stunned to watch people come into the gym without a clipboard. If you are not carrying a clipboard with paper and a pen, and writing down all of your exercise numbers and results, you are absolutely wasting your time. How do you know what you accomplished the last time you worked out, so that you can set the goal to make progress? How do you know what weight you should set the machines to?

Since the primary goal is to beat our numbers every time by either increasing our reps or our weight on the exercise, you can only do this accurately by writing the numbers down and tracking your progress. As well, writing your numbers down allows you to see how you are doing over a period of several weeks or months. If you change the exercises and a few weeks later you want to come back to doing something, it's really handy to know where you left off. For instance, let's say you were doing dumbbell curls with free weights in order to exercise your biceps, then you switched to preacher curls with a padded armrest and a bar, then you switched to a machine instead of free weights… at this point, several months may have gone by, and if you want to cycle back and start doing free weight dumbbell lifts again you probably won't remember how much weight you were lifting.

Even if you are doing a similar exercise, if you change machines, you slightly change the exercise. For example, you might be doing a bench press, but the angle of the machine might be inclined slightly differently, the weights may go up at a different angle, the seat may be positioned slightly closer or father from the bar… you get the idea. Any number of variables comes into play, and you have to write all of these variables down. As soon as one of these variables changes, you've changed the exercise. So remember to write down all of the settings you use on the machine as well. If the seat can be adjusted up or down, make a note on your clip board "Seat set at level #3" (as an example). This way you can accurately recreate the exact same conditions next week.

Use A Strategic Rep Range

There is a real philosophy behind the number of times you lift a weight, or the number of 'reps' that you do. To understand this philosophy it's important to have a little background understanding the different types of muscle that we have in our body.

We have two main types of muscle: Fast-twitch and slow-twitch. Fast twitch muscles fibers are very powerful and allow for an explosive movement, but they can't sustain this effort and they fatigue rapidly. Slow-twitch muscles are really good at endurance exercise, for example running long distances, but they don't have a lot of power. Slow-twitch muscles are typically red in colour because they are rich with oxygen, allowing for aerobic endurance activity. Fast-twitch muscle fibers are typically white in colour, an affect caused by the anaerobic nature of their muscular activity. They don't consume a lot of oxygen compared to red muscle fibers, but because of the anaerobic nature of their muscular contraction they tire quite quickly.

So, what does this have to do with the number of reps that you choose to perform in any given exercise? Think about it: if you do a very light weight, and lift it lots of times, you are doing aerobic exercise and using your red or slow-twitch muscle fibers. However, when you lift a very heavy weight only a few times, you are doing anaerobic exercise and targeting your white or fast-twitch muscle fibers. High-rep and low-weight exercises tend to "tone" muscle, while low-rep and high-weight exercises tend to "build" big muscles.

Because of this, if your goal is to build muscle mass, it has been my experience and the experience of Tom Kiatipis that a general rep range of 8-12 reps is optimal for muscular growth. With leg exercises including squats and leg extensions, we find that a rep range of 10-20 reps can be appropriate as part of your routine as well. If you just want to tone, a higher rep range is usually appropriate.

Exercise To The Point Of Failure

"The last three or four reps is what makes the muscle grow. This area of pain divides the champion from someone else who is not a champion. That's what most people lack, having the guts to go on and just say they'll go through the pain no matter what happens."
- Arnold Schwarzenegger

"Failure" is a term used in the gym to describe the point in your set where you cannot lift the weight any more. (A set is a series of repetitions; for example, 8, 9 or 10 repetitions of lifting dumb bells would constitute one "set" of dumb bells.) When I say you can't lift it, I don't mean that you are tired, or that it has become "uncomfortable". What I mean is that if your very life depended on it, you absolutely couldn't lift the weight even a single time more. If I were to pay you one million dollars, you still could not lift the weight even one more time. This level of absolute exhaustion is called "failure" and is critical to muscle growth.

At this point, you have utterly exhausted the muscle and "broken it down". This means that you've strategically caused the microscopic tears in the muscle fiber required to initiate an adaptive repair response so that the next morning, you wake up with bigger and stronger muscles.

Now, what I see in the gym is that people invariably throw in the towel when they are tired or uncomfortable. When we exercise, our muscles become increasingly fatigued and, as people reach failure, the feeling becomes excruciating. This is commonly attributed to lactic acid buildup in the muscles, although research is starting to contradict this widely held belief.

However, the whole point is to reach the stage where you push your muscles past their previous best effort so that they are forced to adapt and grow. When you are doing 10 reps in an exercise set, the rep that matters the most is the FINAL rep. Every other rep is a warm-up to fatigue the muscle and get you to the point where you break through your previous best effort. However, because of the discomfort involved, people invariably stop at rep number 6, 7 or 8. You don't achieve growth that way! You must push through the discomfort and go to failure in order to maximize your effort. To remind myself of this, I love to wear a sweatshirt in the gym that says "Losers quit when they're tired… winners quit when they've WON."

Using this strategy, it is largely unnecessary to do multiple sets of exercises. I see that people do multiple sets because they are trying to reach the same goal as me: they are trying to exhaust their muscle in order to force adaptation and growth. However, think about the inefficiency of this strategy. You do a light set, then a second set, then a third… building up to the fourth set where you really give it your all and break down the muscle. Why didn't you just give it your all on the first set and save yourself 10 minutes per exercise and leave over an hour early? It's silly to spend hours in the gym. (Tangentially, another way of saving time in the gym is to take shorter breaks between exercises. Increase your intensity and get the job done faster. Don't dilly-dally by wasting time hanging around the water cooler.)

Just do one set to absolute failure, and call it a day for that muscle group. You can fly through an entire workout in under an hour, 30 minutes if you take no breaks.

Fuel Your Body Immediately

It is imperative that right after you work out, you provide your body the raw materials necessary for repairing and rebuilding damaged muscle tissue. That raw material is protein. Since your body is in a resource-depleted state when you finish working out, you've got nothing left in your stomach to aid in post-workout repair and adaptation. Unfortunately, this is the moment when your body needs it the most. The fastest way to get the protein you require, in my opinion, is having a protein shake. There are lots of different shakes in the market, so I'd recommend that you experiment with a few to find one that tastes good and meets your needs. As my coach says, *"If you don't eat at the end of the workout, you've wasted your time."*

> *"If you don't eat at the end of the workout, you've wasted your time."*
> **-Tom Kiatipis**

Muscles Grow When You Rest

As Bill Phillips says, muscles don't grow while you exercise, they grow when you rest. Exercising breaks your muscles down; resting and sleeping gives them a chance to repair, adapt and rebuild so that they are stronger and better than before. Because of this, you must give your muscles a chance to rest. Once you've worked out, wait 48 hours before exercising the same muscles again. For example, if you exercise your biceps on Monday, wait until Wednesday to exercise your biceps again.

If you don't follow this advice, you just break your muscles down Tuesday, and then Wednesday, and then again Thursday... when do your muscles get a chance to rest and repair? They won't, and the impact of your workout will be diminished or erased. Try not to plan any strenuous activity right after working out, since you'll be exhausted and you ruin your muscle growth. For example, if you know you are moving on Saturday and have to lift a lot of heavy boxes and furniture, maybe it's not a good idea to work out Friday night or Saturday morning! (I'm using this example because I've learned this lesson the hard way!)

POINTS TO CONSIDER

Exercise Your Muscles, Not Your Ego

"If you want to be strong, conquer yourself."
- German Proverb

My good friend Kevin Kooger says *"Exercise your muscles, not your ego"*. He usually says this right after I've had sloppy form on one of my exercises! What he means by this statement is that as a team, my friends and I who work out together are very focused on our numbers. So focused, in fact, that the goal becomes "improve your numbers" and silently to ourselves, we say "... at any cost". We are trying to feed our ego by showing that our numbers went up, but we aren't in the gym to exercise our ego. When someone is feeding their ego, they will usually "accidentally" use sloppy form. Here is what I mean. Let's suppose you are doing bicep curls. When you start to fatigue, it becomes harder to lift the weight. In order to continue lifting the weight (and beat your numbers), people will shift their body position by leaning forwards or backward through the range of the exercise, and use momentum to artificially hurl the weights upwards.

Because of this, by working out in teams in Tom's gym we have spotters watching our form as well as cheering us on. When we start to reach failure, we will call out for help. The spotter helps us by assisting in lifting the weights with us, thereby decreasing the weight. When we track our numbers, we call this extra rep "+1". It means that it was an assisted rep. It's purpose is to ensure that we don't compromise our form and that we squeeze every last bit of effort out of our muscles.

Free Weights vs. Machines

A fairly common question is "Should I use free weights or Machines?" Both have strengths and weaknesses. First, let me explain the difference using the bench press as an example. When you do a bench press using free weights, you cannot use as heavy a weight because the added dimension of the exercise is that you are not just lifting the weight straight up and down, you must hold the weight in a steady position as it moves up and down. The bar can't swing too far above your head, too far toward your belt, and both arms must exert the same amount of effort in order to keep the bar level. This requires more than just your pectoral muscles (the large muscles on your chest that are engaged in this exercise). You must also use stabilizing muscles in your shoulders and arms to keep the bar steady. If one arm can lift more than the other, when you are using free weights you will lift according to the weaker arm, since it is the weak link in the chain.

Finally, there is an extra distraction of the potential danger of injury with this exercise: if you reach failure and drop the weight, you're going to drop it right on your face. That hurts if the weight is 10 lbs. But if you're lifting 200 lbs, you have a major problem if you drop it on your face. Therefore, you must be exercising with a friend who will "spot" you; this means they will stand ready to grab the bar on your last rep and help you lower it safely down. Therefore, you can't do the exercise properly if you are alone.

So, why do so many people advocate free weights over machines? Because the variability of the movement produces greater results. When you do a bench press on a machine, it lifts straight up and down. When you do this exercise using free weights, the bar naturally wobbles and drifts a little forward and backward. This slightly varies the muscles that are being engaged, hitting more of the muscle fibers in your pectoral muscle. So instead of just exercising the middle of your pectoral muscles (or "pecs"), you are exercising more of the top and the bottom as well.

Many people are advocates of JUST using free weights, but I believe in using both. I think machines have some tremendous advantages as I've described above. Because the exercise follows the exact range of motion on each rep, you can't slack off and adjust your position during the exercise to artificially increase the number of reps that you do. The machine forces you to use better form more consistently than free weights. You don't need a spotter for safety (although it always helps to have a cheering team!)

Have A Jogging Buddy

Human nature consistently shows that willpower fades and internal motivation fluctuates based upon our energy level, emotional state, physical comfort level, etc. Don't count on willpower to get you in the gym; count on your team. It is a really good idea work out with a friend. When you don't want to work out, you can be motivated by your commitment to keep your appointment and promise to them. After all, they really need you too! Not only that, you might slack off and not push yourself to failure; your friend can cheer you on and push you to go ever longer and workout even harder. I can tell you that many, many times I have not wanted to workout when I have it scheduled. And the only thing that gets me out the door to the gym is my commitment to my coach and friends.

Additionally, many times I want to throw in the towel and go home early because I'm exhausted and our workouts are so incredibly grueling. If I didn't have my friends there, I guarantee that I would cut out sooner. When you are exhausted and facing another 30 minutes of incredibly intense exercise, willpower evaporates. Now it's just an issue of character; can you stay the course and finish what you started?
(*Note: choose your workout buddy carefully! Make sure that they are someone who is absolutely committed to success, because if they choose to slack off they will drag you down!)

Be Wary of Trainers

It's quite common for people to get motivated about changing their body; invariably they feel that they will be extra-motivated if they go to their gym and hire a personal trainer. And it's true: you definitely benefit having someone push you past where you want to go, and especially if they are experienced and know how to get results.

> *Every fitness program needs a combination of diet, cardio and weight training. Leaving any part of this out is like removing one leg from a tripod; the whole structure collapses.*
> **-CJ Calvert**

However, let me be very clear: as much as a trainer may want to help you, they have a mortgage to pay and a family to feed. And you are their meal ticket. A savvy trainer will be charismatic, experienced, motivational… and refuse to reveal their secrets. You will walk away from most fitness trainers having learned almost nothing. You will have no idea how to replicate anything they've taught you, because there won't be an obvious pattern or system that they are following. Each workout will be radically different from the last workout, and they will surprise you each session with a new "advanced" technique. The purpose of doing this is very simple: they want you to be absolutely dependant on them. You see, if you learn how to crack the code of exercise, you won't need them, and they are out of business.

So, insist on a written weekly program of exercises. Insist that you repeat this program exactly for several weeks in a row. Eventually your muscles will stop adapting (after 6-8 weeks) and you will need to change the exercises to shock your muscles; this is called "periodization". But you should not be changing the exercises every week. Your instructor might have a slightly different program for Tuesday, and then a slightly different program for Saturday. That's absolutely fine. But next Tuesday, you had better be repeating the same exercises you did last week, writing your numbers down on a clipboard and then setting the goal of beating your numbers. If you aren't, then you've got a trainer who is toying with you and making you dependant on them. This doesn't mean that they are a bad person or out to hurt you; it just means that they are focused on making money first and foremost.

As well, every fitness program needs a combination of diet, cardio and weight training. Leaving any part of this out is like removing one leg from a tripod; the whole structure collapses. You must do all three things to have success!

BURNING FAT

Cardio: HIIT It!

In his fantastic book "Absolution", author and bodybuilder Shawn Phillips highlighted one of his key strategies to staying at under 6% body fat. This strategy is called High-Intensity Interval Training, or HIIT. This is a marked departure from the traditional theory that when doing cardio, you should exercise at a moderate rate in order to burn fat.

Understand that when you do cardio, the first 20 minutes are wasted (assuming that you are doing a traditional cardio routine of moderate exertion). What happens is that when you exercise, your body consumes calories as a fuel source. The most immediate fuel source is glucose in your blood stream. Roughly speaking, it takes approximately 20 minutes for the average person to burn off all of their available blood sugar before the body begins searching for an alternative fuel source.

That alternative fuel source is FAT. After 20 minutes, you start burning fat. That means that if you run for 21 minutes, you only do one minute of fat-burning. If you run for 30 minutes, you do 10 minutes of fat-burning. After you get off of the treadmill, your body temperature and heart rate are elevated, and you will continue a very small amount of extra fat-burning over the next few hours.

If you use this strategy, you have to stay on the treadmill for at least an hour if you want to see some serious results. And I mean an hour every single day, for 12 weeks. No offense to the proponents of this particular strategy, but I frankly don't have that amount of time that I choose to invest. Given the choice, wouldn't you prefer a much more efficient strategy at fat-burning?

This is where HIIT comes into play. After a reasonable stretch and warming up (at your discretion), what you do is you SPRINT, as fast as humanly possible, for 60 seconds. Then you drop the treadmill (or the bike or elliptical machine; whatever you are using) to a moderate pace for 60 seconds and you jog. Then, you SPRINT again for 60 seconds, flat-out. Then, you jog for 60 seconds. Repeat this process for 16-20 minutes; that is all that is necessary.

Here is what happens. As I mentioned before, you don't burn any fat in the first 20 minutes, so you won't burn fat while you are doing HIIT. Because of this, many people erroneously dismiss this as anaerobic exercise and ignore the strategic benefit. It is true that you are working the white muscle fibers in your legs and pushing yourself to the limit. You are definitely adapting to intense exertion. But it doesn't matter that you don't burn any fat during HIIT. What matters is that because of the extreme intensity of your exertion, your body temperature and your metabolism are forced through the roof. You begin heating up like a furnace, and this internal furnace keeps burning when you get off the machine. So what happens is you burn fat *all day long*. You burn fat driving your car to work, sitting at your desk, watching TV at home and sleeping in your bed. Your body becomes a fat-burning machine and your heightened metabolism begins shedding fat aggressively.

I'm not just sharing theory with you here, this is exactly what I did to get to 4.6% body fat in March of 2006, and then down to 2.98% body fat for my first bodybuilding competition on stage in May 2008. You don't need to set such extreme goals, and you shouldn't aim for these goals unless you have a professionally accredited fitness coach monitoring your progress. It is simply not healthy to maintain body fat levels at such a low level, and you really only do it for fitness competitions. I'm sharing these numbers with you to show that this technique yields MASSIVE results. Simply use the technique along with everything else I'm telling you here, and when you create the body fat levels you want you can ease up on the cardio.

The Myth of Low-Carb Diets

In the last few years, we've heard a lot of negative press about carbs. Many low-carb diets have sprung up and claimed success in helping people achieve their diet and weight-loss goals. The reason that these diets are so popular is that they WORK: people lose weight. However, what people don't realize is the long-term problem they are creating, and what the diet is actually doing to your body.

You see, carbohydrates are the gasoline in your blood stream. They are literally the fuel that powers your body's metabolic processes. You cannot live without carbs. If you cut carbs out of your diet and your blood sugar level goes down, your body has to find sugar somewhere else. The popular belief is that your body begins converting fat back into energy to power your body. This is the function of fat, but your body doesn't go after fat first. When faced with a lack of energy, your body breaks down muscle first as a source of immediate energy. Your body breaks muscle fibers back down into their original amino acids and converts the amino acid to glucose.

What's the problem with this? Muscles consume calories. Losing muscle mass causes your body's caloric consumption to decrease and your metabolism goes down with it. For every pound of additional muscle, you burn more calories. (Incidentally, this is one of the reasons that a proper diet plan includes building muscle and not just cutting out junk food. More muscle means you burn more calories all day long). When you lose muscle you have extra calories NOT being burned… and they get stored as FAT. This is the opposite of what you want to have happen.

Many people don't notice that they are losing muscle because the scale in their bathroom tells them that they've lost weight. Don't ever set the goal of losing weight; if you want to change your body shape, set the goal of losing fat and building muscle. Muscle is denser than fat, and so you may actually weigh MORE after building muscle. This can be quite confusing for people, when the number on the scale goes UP but their dress size goes DOWN! Ignore the scale; for almost everyone it's just a ridiculous distraction.

Don't CUT Carbs, Just Manage Your Portions

"To lengthen thy Life, lessen thy meals."
- Benjamin Franklin

Continuing on the vein of low-carb diets, the existence of these diets is a reaction of the pendulum swinging too far to one side. Since carbs are converted to glucose, they are just a glorified junk food when taken in excessive quantity. They require less effort to eat and they taste great. Protein has a layer of nitrogen that must be stripped before it can be broken down in our stomach and digestive tract, which adds an additional metabolic step and therefore requires more energy to digest. Because of this, it's easier to eat pasta than it is to eat steak.

Many people are becoming aware of the concept of managing your portions. What this means is that you get clear on how much carbs you eat in relation to how much protein, and fat. **For every 7 grams of protein you consume, you should eat 9 grams of complex carbs, and one gram of good quality fat** (like almond butter, for example). Fat is a necessary part of your diet for proper brain function and metabolic processes and should NOT be cut out completely; it just needs to be portioned correctly. So, if you have a 42-gram chicken breast, you should have 54 grams of complex carbs (potatoes, for example) and 6 grams of quality fat.

Have A "Free" Meal

I advocate a weekly meal called a "free" meal. This is a meal where you can eat anything you want! You can eat pizza, potato chips, ice cream, beer… whatever your heart desires. What is the point of this?

When you diet, your body might think that you are in a dangerous situation (such as being lost in the forest) and you don't have adequate food. When your body senses a food shortage and the onset of starvation, your metabolism will be slowed in order to consume fewer calories. Any food you eat is meted out very carefully and fat is stored aggressively for the tough days ahead. This is a really good reaction if you are actually in a situation where you face starvation. It is NOT a good reaction if you are trying to lose weight. In fact, when people under-eat on a diet they artificially drive their metabolism down. When they inevitably come off the diet and go back to their old eating habits, the same food consumption will put on much more fat because their body's metabolism has switched over to storing fat instead of burning it! This is one of the major problems of yo-yo diets that people start and stop. It plays havoc with your metabolism.

To combat this, have a "free meal" each week. When you pig out on junk food, it confuses your body and shows that you are not in a starvation situation. As well, food has a powerful psychological power. People often eat food in times of high stress as a tool to manage their emotions; this is called "comfort food" and is usually high-carbs or junk food. When people go on a strict diet and cut off all of their favorite junk foods, they might actually feel depressed and feel a sense of loss from cutting off all of the chocolate in their life, for example. A free meal helps combat depression in this case.

Finally, it can be socially challenging to stick to a diet when you visit your family on the weekend and have the big family dinner or Holiday dinner. You might feel guilty not eating your Mom's great cooking, especially since she's been slaving over a hot stove all day in anticipation of your arrival. Being able to use your "free meal" on a night with a big family dinner allows you an opportunity to avoid the tension of saying no to your Mom's great cooking, and it gives you a chance to enjoy the dinner without guilt. People sometimes feel so guilty when they break their diet that they give up completely and come off the diet! By building a "free meal" into your diet, you can eat what you want on Saturday and not feel like you've failed and let yourself down. This is a much more realistic strategy and having a free meal helps people stay on their diet more successfully.

ACTION STEPS

1. **Make the decision to change**. What are all of the benefits you will enjoy when you transform your fitness level? What will the consequences be if you don't take action? Put your thoughts down on paper and create a pros and cons list to help motivate yourself.
2. Visit www.personalcoachprogram.com to check out information on how to develop your personalized meal plan and to connect with Canada's #1 fitness coach, Tom Kiatipis
3. **Take action today!** Do one pushup today! Do a sit up, jumping jack, or climb an extra flight of stairs. Even it is a small step, don't put it off. Increase your activity level until you reach a point that you will yield results, as determined in consultation with your coach.
4. **Track everything you eat.** This includes snacks, juice, water, salt, butter that you put on your bread... absolutely everything. What you are eating should tell you the story. You don't need to read a book on healthy cooking to know that you shouldn't be eating candy bars, soda pop and potato chips every day.
5. Go through you cupboards and fridge with a garbage bag in your hand, and **THROW AWAY any junk food in your home.** This includes anything in a wrapper, anything with

cartoon-characters on the box, etc. If you've got kids who are eating this stuff, you may need to hold a family meeting. Be wary of hidden carbs in condiments like Caesar salad dressing, ketchup, juice, butter, etc. Switch over to low-fat dressing like balsamic or raspberry vinaigrette, or mustard instead of ketchup. Crackers, cookies, popcorn, potato chips… all of these high-carb snacks that can be munched on easily need to go.

6. **Set a fun reward** for each week over the next month for 7 consecutive days of following a fitness and diet plan. Reward yourself in the beginning for accomplishing activity goals… soon you will switch over and reward yourself only for result goals. But in the beginning, get some momentum by doing the right things each day. Proper daily habits will yield proper results.
7. **Have fun!** You're on your way to dramatically improving your health and creating the body of your dreams!

CONCLUSION

Congratulations! Reaching the end of any book is a significant accomplishment: you are one of the rare and exceptional people who finish what they start. Many people begin a task; the world is in great need of more people like yourself who stay focused and complete the work at hand.

As you reflect on the strategies I have shared with you, please remember this: despite popular opinion to the contrary, knowledge is *not* power. The *application* of knowledge is power. Reading any self-improvement book is a good first step, but if you don't take action on what you've learned you have wasted your time.

> ***Knowledge is* not *power. The* application *of knowledge is power.***
> -CJ Calvert

Decide, right now, what one thing you are going to change today. What will you do differently so that our time together has been a powerful investment in your future?

Will you…

- Choose to have a **positive attitude** by asking "what's positive about this?" the next time you are in a lineup that is running too long, or laugh at your own absurd frustrations?
- Choose to **reduce stress** by breathing deeply and calming down the next time you feel the pressure mounting?

- Choose to **manage your time** more effectively by starting your day doing the most important thing first?
- Choose to determine your destiny by **setting goals**, writing them down and applying rewards and consequences to motivate you to hit your deadline?
- Choose to draw inspiration from the courageous individuals who have **overcome obstacles** in their lives, so that their example can mobilize you when you feel discouraged?
- Choose to find a jogging buddy and become accountable to a friend as you pursue your goal of increased **health, fitness and vitality?**

If you follow through on these commitments to yourself, you will transform your life forever. You will completely redesign your daily life experience so dramatically, that within days or weeks you will feel alive, energized and fully engaged in all of your endeavors. Life will be fun. You will wake up each morning, and instead of grumbling… you will feel grateful. Each day is a precious gift that is given to us, and it is in our hands to make it a masterpiece.

I wish you all of the success that you are willing to work for!

With love and respect,
CJ Calvert

Notes